獻給所有的爹爹奶奶

Dedicated to all Grandmas and Grandpas

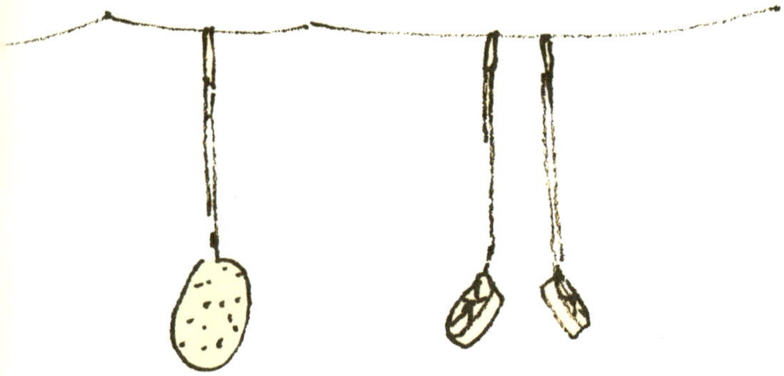

老爹媽思厨
GRANDMA GRANDPA COOK

mccmcreations

珍惜身邊人
CHERISH THOSE AROUND YOU

符榮師 MIG FU

還記得上次吃祖母親手弄的菜餚是幾時嗎？記得兒時吃過祖母弄的紫砂碗蒸肉片，留香至今。有紫砂與豬肉的香味，更有深厚的人情味。人不在，味常在，情永在。

我們與長者一起製作美食，分享美食，更透過戲劇、音樂、影像及舞蹈分享人生。

每一道菜都是一個人生故事：「鮮奶粟米雞湯」的童年放牛回憶、「家常便飯蒸肉餅」的戰爭與和平、三年零八個月的人生芝麻糊、一家鍾愛的「甜甜蜜蜜比翼雙飛」……

每個人都有自己的一道菜。珍惜這道菜，更珍惜身邊人。

Remember the last time you ate something made by grandma?

I can still recall the aroma of the Steamed Pork Slices in Zisha Bowl my grandma made. It was luscious with affection. The person is gone, but the taste of love remains.

We cooked with the grandmas and grandpas in this book and shared the food. We even shared our lives through drama, music, video and dance.

Every dish is a story of life—Milky Chicken Corn Soup and childhood memories of tending cattle, Steamed Pork Cake entangled in war and peace, Sesame Sweet Soup and life during the Three Years and Eight Months (of the Japanese occupation of Hong Kong), Sweety Honey Paired Chicken Wings that the whole family loves…

Everyone has a favourite dish. Cherish the dish, cherish those around you.

食物由人所做，也為人而做，所以無可避免地滲透著人的生活、文化、記憶和歷史。

食物的身體記憶

小西

要談食物跟生活、文化、記憶與歷史的關聯，最經典的莫過於法國小說家普魯斯特（Marcel Proust）在其巨構《追憶似水年華》（la recherche du temps perdu）中，提到的一個有關「小瑪德蓮娜蛋糕」（petite madeleine）的小故事：在一個凜冽的冬夜，小說的主角馬塞爾回到家中，母親送上熱茶和小瑪德蓮娜蛋糕。他沒有胃口並不想吃，但隨即改變了心意，舀了一勺泡著蛋糕的茶，在送入口中的片刻，味覺的感受勾起了昔日的回憶，使他想起童年時在萊奧妮姨媽家裡的情形。為了重拾過往的記憶，他再次品嚐，然而他卻再想不起什麼。當他放棄不再回想的時候，昔日貢布雷的景象，突然之間從熟悉的茶點氣味中迸發而出。

不錯，食物每每跟人的生活記憶交纏在一起，難解難分，因為人的生活記憶本身，更多的時候是在人的無意識層面上運作。有些時候，有些舊事（尤其是令人傷痛的遙遠舊事）可能連當事人自身都以為早已忘掉了，但往往是一件表面看來毫不起眼但又似曾相識的物件、食物、風景，甚至路人的一個不經意的手勢，突然之間讓昔日的回憶自身體的某個角落，不請自來。而且過去的景象總是如在目前，但又明知早已不在了。若果讓人勾起生活回憶的是一片小小的蛋糕，當曾經有過的那甜自身體的深處昇起，口中的那甜便彷彿不再一樣：跟記憶中的那甜相比，當下口中的那甜是差遠了，但正正是口中的那甜，更突顯記憶中那令人回味的味道的逝去。差了些什麼呢？可能是一個人、一種生活方式，甚至是一片早已不再存在的風景。

在這一本有關食物、生活、文化和記憶的小書中，透過公公婆婆的口述，我們勉力嘗試重構一個又一個有關食物的生活故事。在消費主義當道的年代，希望讓讀者能夠有機會從作為物件的食物，嘗試回到一個被遮蔽了的價值與人文的世界。但在那被複述的記憶中，就算再具體與充滿生活的細節，被複述的記憶也只能是抽象的。我們能切身體會好像馬塞爾在品嚐一片小蛋糕時那種「瞬間閃念」的感受嗎？所以，這同時也是一本悼亡書，除了哀悼幾位在本書書成之前仙逝的長者外，也追悼那種註定無法還原的身體記憶與感受。傳統的家教，會強調「身教」的重要性，除了所謂「以身作則」的道德調教外，我相信更貼身的「身教」，往往來自一些表面看來毫不起眼的共同身體記憶，它的媒介或載體，可以是一件小玩具、一支老歌，也可能是一片吃了一半，擱在小書桌上的雲片糕。

讀王維詩作《相思》：「紅豆生南國，春來發幾枝，勸君多採擷，此物最相思」，我們往往會把「紅豆」看作「相思」的象徵。但有時我會俏皮的想：若果對方真的聽詩中主角的意見，多採下來的紅豆，又得到怎樣的發落呢？它們會否變成一碗美味的紅豆沙？當對方每次品嚐平凡不過的紅豆沙，那種自身體深處、不由自主地滲透出的相思感，大概只有當事人「冷暖自知」了！

THE BODY REMEMBERS

TINY WEST

The relation of food with life, culture, memory and history is best exemplified in Marcel Proust's great work *À la recherche du temps perdu*. Proust tells the story of the petite Madeleine. On a bleak, cold winter night, Marcel, the protagonist of the novel returns home. His mother makes him hot tea and a petite Madeleine, which he at first, doesn't feel like eating. But in the next instant, he changes his mind. He dips the cake into the tea and has a sip. Instantly, memories of his childhood at his auntie's house comes surging back. To capture these memories, he has another sip, but to no avail. One day, he decides to give up, but the familiar taste of the tea brings endless images of the old village of Combray.

It is true that food and memories are intertwined, because memories often work on the unconscious levels of daily life. At times, past events (especially the most hurting ones from a distant past) that the person thinks he/she had long forgotten, come back to life in the most trivial encounter with things, food, landscape, even a small gesture of a passing stranger. Like uninvited guests to a party, memories pop out of some corner of the body. The past, long lost, is brought to the present. When a little piece of cake evokes memories of life, the sweet taste that arises out of the depth of the body's memory is often far more profound than the immediate sweetness of the present. Yet it is also the present that amplifies the loss of the past. What could have filled this gap? Perhaps a person, a way of life, or a scene that has long disappeared.

This book is about food, life, culture and memory. As grandpas and grandmas speak about food, we try to re-construct their stories of life. We hope that readers can recover a world hidden behind consumerism, a world of humanity. Yet, however detailed memories are, they are always abstract. Can we share the flashback that Marcel experienced when he had the cake? This is why this book is also a book of mourning—for the grannies who passed away since the beginning of this project, and also the bodily memories and emotions that can never be restored to their original shape. Traditional education within the family has always emphasized the importance of "body teaching," that is, setting a good example by practice. I believe that an even more intimate way of body teaching begins from shared bodily memories that may be too trivial to catch the eye—from a small piece of a toy to an old tune, or even a piece of half-eaten *wen pian gao*, laying on the small work desk.

Wang Wei's poem *Longing* (Xiang Si) says, "red beans grow in the south / spring has them budding out / pick more of them for the gentlemen / they are a remembrance of longing." We tend to take "red beans" as a symbol of longing. But I like to think of them in a naughty way. If we really follow the poem's instruction and pick a lot of red beans, what could happen? Would they not become a tasty bowl of sweet red bean soup? When someone has a taste of this ordinary soup, a sense of longing comes oozing out from the depths of the body. Only that person will know whether it feels warm or cold.

FOOD IS MADE BY THE PEOPLE AND FOR THE PEOPLE. IT INEVITABLY EXUDES LIVES, CULTURES, MEMORIES AND HISTORIES.

味覺拾遺

小土

McDonald's是一個帝國。這個軍隊拿著「快」劍與「廉」盾，加上「多元化」暗器、「優惠」鎖鏈、品牌陣法等等，統佔全球飲食業。有不少學者已對 McDonald's 作出不少研究。無論如何，McDonald's 已成為餐飲業發展的一個里程碑，飲食文化演義中不可不提的情節。在這裡不是要分析 McDonald's 如何如何成功／敗壞，值得注意的是其昌盛並非偶然。社會學家韋伯（Max Weber）指出現代社會其中一項重要特徵就是講求效率的工具理性。McDonald's 正契合此時代的精神而得以速成。

當然這只是一面之詞，複雜的現象總有許多其他解釋，視乎言者站於何種立場。文化之多樣，又豈可一概而論。與快餐巨浪抗衡的 Slow Food 也是一場不可忽視的社會運動。此書的立意或多或少與此沾上邊兒。再者，除Mc效應外，我們的飲食文化中更有精緻品味的追求。由「米芝蓮」（Michelin）星級定位到私房菜的同好歡聚，從烹調的藝術到進餐氣氛的營造，那亦是我們生活中不可輕視的內在價值。在此不是說「快」一定不好，我就不時會以「麥樂卡」購買麥記套餐，貪多一件贈送的蘋果批或雪糕新地。趕上班時，更會外賣一份套餐在乘車時進食，好像很需要麥記。當然我永不會忘懷曾享用的法國大餐，每一道菜就像珍珠般閃爍，輕撫味蕾。那滋味就是一種藝術美。（花了成千元當然好食？）

食，自有其功能，也可有其內在的要求，但仍有一種價值、一種立場、一種態度、一種味道，是我們甚或忽視，逐漸消失，幾近遺忘。尚有一種構成我們文化不可或缺，甚至身分認同的一種味覺，是必需保留且需不斷更新的。不是要說什麼「集體回憶」。最怕的是，所謂回憶好像只需有文字記錄又或（立體）相片存影，甚至流動錄像，就能好好封存。想要指出的是，會不會有些事兒是不可分割地構成一個整體、一種飲食、一種文化？而不以這種烹調方法、這類材料，就不能再現這種滋味，維繫這樣的健康生態。這正是本書所期望努力的實踐成果。其實梅菜扣肉配碟飯不會很肥，肥肉連瘦肉一口咬下那種感覺是難以形容的美妙滿足，偶爾又會憶起第一次舅父牽我出外吃這碟飯時的溫情。

杜甫《北征》說得好：

或紅如丹砂　或黑如點漆
雨露之所濡　甘苦齊結實

味道是有歷史的。一道菜正是一個故事，其烹調、選料、味道，盛載歷史勾起回憶之餘，更體現著一種文化。我們固然有宏觀的偉大敍事作共同背景，但個人的參與創造的小事，也是不可或缺的變奏。而這種歷史、這種味道就在這道菜、這個地方，混然一體，構成一種價值。我們的回憶、我們的身分認同就維繫於此時此地。這點與皇后天星碼頭運動所爭取的是一致的，遷移了的那只是一個分離的標本。以上所論的價值觀或許未必盡為同意，可再作討論。但是我們最大的悲哀，莫過於尚未對話，已然結束；不曾確定，已被摧毀。

本人有幸得嚐書中好些長者所烹煮的窩心小吃，亦有幸聽到他們的繞樑歌聲，親歷他們的調皮活力。三幸，本人能夠編輯此書，細味他們那勇於承擔、敢於挑戰、安於動盪、常存盼望、奮發創新的精神，萬分感恩。可惜，愚生不才，錯漏之處，懇請指正賜教。另外，本人實在疏懶，有的長者已經仙遊未及看到成書，在此深表歉意。還望你亦能享受到這場盛宴之一二。

GLEANING TASTE

SIU TO

McDonald's restaurant is an empire. It boasts an army equipped with (fast) swords and (cheap) shields, secret weapons like "diversity" and "chain promotion", branding strategies and more. Many scholars have studied the McDonald's phenomenon, which is seen as a landmark in the development of the food and catering industry. It is a name that any discussion on the evolution of food culture cannot miss. A century ago, sociologist Max Weber identified rationalization as the main feature of modern societies. McDonald's is definitely a product of its times.

This is, however, an over-simplification—there are many reasons behind complex phenomena. Culture in its diversity can never be explained by one theory. Consider Slow Food, which counters the fast food tide and has gradually become a significant cultural movement. This book has a similar intention. Moreover, food culture also includes the quest for fine taste. From Michelin restaurants to "private kitchens", we share not only the art of cooking, but also hearty moments with friends that make the fabric of our lives. Sometimes, even going "fast" can be a value. Once in a while, I use my McDonald's membership card to buy set meals because I get an apple pie or ice-cream sundae for free. When I am in a hurry, I grab a meal-to-go and eat it on the bus. It seems I can't live without McDonald's. And then there is also the French cuisine I can never forget. Every course is a glistening pearl, gently fondling my taste buds. It is the taste of art. (It had better be good because I spent more than $1,000, on the meal!)

Food has its function, but also its intrinsic values. And there is also one aspect of it—an approach, an attitude, a flavor, that we have ignored, and may be disappearing. This aspect of food is integral to our cultural identity. It must be preserved and constantly rejuvenated. Memories of food require not just textual or photographic documentation because food is one of those things in life that is whole—it comes to life only with specific ingredients cooked in specific ways, constituting a particular state of well-being. This is precisely what this book seeks to do. The fatty meat in Preserved Vegetables and Fatty Meat is actually not so fatty—imagine having both fatty and lean meat in one bite. It feels so wholesome that it is hard to describe. Once in a while, it reminds me of the heartwarming feeling I had when my uncle took me out to try this dish for the first time.

Taste has a history. Every dish tells a story. These are intertwined with the way it is cooked and the ingredients used. This is a culture. Grand, big stories link us together; small stories are also essential. It is when the history and taste of this place are blended in one dish that a value is formed.

I was very fortunate to have tried some of the heart-warming dishes made by the grandmas and grandpas featured in this book. I have also danced and sang with them. Above all, I am deeply grateful for the opportunity to be the Chinese Editor of this book, their book. I have learned a lot from their courage, sense of responsibility, calmness in turmoil, perseverance and inventive spirit. On this note, I must also confess that because of my slackness, some of the people here passed away and will never have the chance to see this book. I would like to express my sincere apology.

Here is a feast for you to remember.

訪梁以瑚

土 | 中文編輯小土
瑚 | 計劃統籌人梁以瑚女士

這天就像昨天，如常晴朗。聽著大家暱稱她「二胡婆婆」的梁以瑚說起這本書的許多小故書。

土 | 這個計劃是怎樣形成的？
瑚 | 這是我們服務南亞裔和聾啞「至叻美猴王」計劃以後的新發展。我們關心香港的弱勢社群，一直探索有哪些社群是我們可以接觸到的。起初曾考慮失業中年男士，後來想到可能與社區中心合作效果會更好，因為他們已有固定的服務，那就不用從零開始。我的朋友阿Mig就在鄰舍輔導會轄下的社區中心服務長者，他表示很歡迎，我們就立刻撰寫計劃書。我們起先是接觸牛頭角下邨社區中心的長者。他們許多已被逼搬遷離開多年的社群，有的就搬往獨居長者的新樓如將軍澳或觀塘，有的仔女已移民不在身邊，不過他們都喜歡回到這個中心見見面。之後我們又延伸至石硤尾的社區中心，期間有許多義工參與服務，有的更帶來自己的家人，就是這樣慢慢延伸開去。

土 | 那為何與食扯上關係呢？
瑚 | 因為我們都喜歡食，喜歡聽老人家說故事。老人家說故事，許多時候會提起食。更經常勸勉我們這些「後生要食多些」，又教我們如何如何補身。不論親疏，也對晚輩十分關愛。這也是中國人一種問安方式。回到家，媽媽總會煮子女喜歡吃的餸菜，這是中國人最簡單表示愛的方式。

可能我也不太願意長大，很小的時候就喜歡親近長輩。那時農曆新年前的年三十晚，我總會陪婆婆一起睡，其他哥哥姐姐不陪。那我就會有「雙封利是」，婆婆會於午夜十二時給我一封，早上起來又有另一封，其他哥哥姐姐就只有一封。最喜歡拖著老人家的手，有時他們會搓搓你的手，就這樣傳情，會感受到他們的關懷，抑鬱或不快的情緒也會慢慢溶化。若他們停止搓你的手，你可以去撫撫他們，回報他們的關心。老人或小孩，也可以這樣互通聲氣的。在與老人家談話中，我也找回曾經與我親近的婆婆、叔叔、爸爸，那份親人的感覺。

開始接觸長者時，不經意地以食物吸引他們。他們說起最珍重的食物時，又會講到自己難忘的經歷。他們對食物的回憶反而成為媒介，引發他們說出自己的故事。他們平日會唱曲搓麻雀，反而不會談到這些故事。有個伯伯很沉默，但一談到小時候如何在田間玩耍，就手舞足蹈，如何挖田啊，又捉什麼什麼，很是興奮。另外一個婆婆更說：「我買鴉片啊！」跟著又示範如何一袋袋背起運走。他們講起走難這些艱辛日子，好像也是很甜蜜的。

土 | 還有哪些趣事？
瑚 | 我們服務期間，還有些原本互不認識的老人家，竟走在一起，出來跳現代舞。有的又好像在談戀愛般如沐春風，當朱伯拉二胡時，整班婆婆圍住他。他們個個回復青春，我們就變成小孩。邊聽故事，邊一齊玩。開頭有的已很熟。九個月來，老人家都很期待我們每個星期二的來臨相聚。我們也好像去領受祝福似的，每次到訪中心，都有很美味的食物等待我們。我們從他們身

INTERVIEW WITH EVELYNA LIANG

T | SIU TO, CHINESE EDITOR

E | EVELYNA LIANG, PROJECT COORDINATOR

T | How did this project take shape?

E | It is an extension of our other projects with South Asian communities and hearing-impaired people in Hong Kong. We have been working with under-privileged people for some time, including middle-aged unemployed men. We realized it's good to work with community centers because we can build on the regular services they provide, rather than starting from scratch. My friend Mig was working with elderly people at the Neighbourhood-Advice Action Council. He liked our idea, so we gave him a proposal. We started working with elderly people at a community center in Ngau Tau Kok Lower Estate. Many of them were no longer residents in the district. They had moved to new buildings for single elderly persons in Tseung Kwan O and Kwun Tong because of urban development in the area. Some of their children had emigrated. Yet, they enjoyed going back to the Ngau Tau Kok community center to meet their friends. Later on, we extended our project to a community center in Shek Kip Mei. Many volunteers began to join. They brought their family members. This is how the project spread.

T | How did the idea of food come in?

E | We all like to eat. We all like to listen to grandmas and grandpas telling stories. When they tell stories, food always comes up as a topic. They always tell us, "young people should eat more", and they teach us how to stay healthy. They take care of younger people even if they are not their relatives, which is quite common in Chinese culture. When we go home to visit our parents, they always prepare our favourite dishes. This is a simple way that Chinese people express love for each other.

I guess I don't really want to grow up. I have always liked to be with older people. As a child, I would sleep with my grandmother on Chinese New Year's Eve. My sisters and brothers wouldn't do that. Grandma would give me double *lai see* (two red packets), one at midnight, and another one on New Year's Day. My brothers and sisters would have only one *lai see*. I love holding the hand of an elderly person. Sometimes they squeeze your hand gently. This is how they communicate loving feelings. I would feel their care, and my sadness would melt. When they stop, you might want to pat them in turn to show your care. Elderly people and children communicate in this subtle way. When I talk with elderly people, I find the same sense of intimacy I used to feel when I was with my grandma, uncle and father.

When I started to get in touch with the grandmas and grandpas in this book, food came up a lot. The food they treasured would be woven with memorable stories of their lives. Memories of food stimulated them to talk about themselves, which they don't do very often in their everyday lives, although they sing and play mahjong together. I remember chatting with

THIS BOOK COMES ABOUT FROM MY LOVE OF FOOD AND LOVE OF STORIES.

上取得很多，要對得起老人家，為他們做些事，所以一定要出版這本書。

土｜成書以前，你們好像就曾以這些故事排演一齣戲。

瑚｜這計劃起初是小西和 Denny Cheng 發起的，他們一想就是演戲。若是我的話，通常就會由視覺藝術出發。起先就以 playback 的形式誘發他們說出對食物的回憶。後來我們以香港這城市的歷史發展作背景，將與他們年代有關的故事串連成一齣戲劇。他們的故事可能很家常，但亦很珍貴，其中不乏我們的集體回憶，例如走難、倒夜香。但有的在今天看來亦匪夷所思，有位婆婆說，曾看到有個人因為太肚餓食起竹葉來，結果死了。

其實我們的製作費不太足夠，要靠很多人幫忙。感謝美麗華酒樓集團的資助，後來有機會在香港文化博物館上演話劇及展覽呢。另外，幸有義工賣力支持，有的更身兼數職。就如Esther本來是做義工，後來又幫忙做演戲道具，現在又幫忙食譜的部分編輯工作。

土｜過程中有很多有心人。

瑚｜差不多每個階段也遇上一些有心人來幫忙。有天我在卑利街附近，遇見一個很古怪的外國人拿著一架很古老的相機在街上走來走去，於是上前攀談，發覺原來他也很「為食」，向他提及這計劃，他就興致勃勃希望替這些老人家拍攝一輯相片。那位先生就是Michael Wolf。

土｜在其中你最大的得著是什麼？

瑚｜最大得益是，我廚藝好了，最重要是重新找回自己的味覺。現在我們可以買到許多現成醬料，但可能對食物的味覺已經變得麻木。老人家常常說不用買現成的，自己做便可以，如豆醬蒸魚要三種醬料混合起來才好吃，一是為豐富食物的質感，一是為調味，一是為賣相，那樣就有原來的味道。我照著他們的方法做，真的由舌尖到舌底都感到美味。

又如他們提起磨芝麻糊要用擂漿棍這樣的東西。香港四處問人都買不到，原來要用堅硬的番石榴木做，返故鄉時發現有人還懂得製作擂漿棍，就替我做了兩根。當我拿那兩根擂漿棍去社區中心，老人家個個十分興奮，立刻搶著要磨給我們看，就好像遇見一個老朋友要show off。我們自己去磨時，發覺真的很難，要用腳那樣夾著沙盤然後運用陰力才行。第二個星期去探訪時就有芝麻糊請我們吃了。之後又有個婆婆說懂得製瀨粉，現在瀨粉是用米粉開水做的，沒有啃口，若要有，就得用冷飯與米粉混合然後用有孔的鐵片擠出來。越是與他們對話，越發現更多失落的味道，好像找到自己失散的一部分。

土｜其實昔日的飲食習慣背後有一套與我們現今文化很不同的價值，我很是嚮往，失傳的話真的很可惜。

瑚｜現代的生活節拍叫我們忙於應付，沒有多少空閒讓人可以靜下來思考。以往沒有那麼多資訊，沒有那麼多誘惑，每樣食物可以慢慢去預備，細心去切。現在看完無線，可以看有線，再看CNN，BCC，CCTV-9台，可以知道許多事情，那些資訊很遙遠很陌生，就算不知那是什麼什麼地方，但仍想知道些什麼。可是那些地方對我來

a very quiet grandpa. When we came to childhood memories, he became excited and talked about how he played in the fields, catching this and that. Another grandma said to me, "I was selling opium!" She would demonstrate how she carried bag after bag of it. It almost felt as if they enjoyed talking about those bitter days.

T | Can you tell us more interesting stories?
E | During the span of our project, elderly people got to know each other; they even danced together. When Grandpa Chu played the erhu, all the grandmas sat around him and listened attentively. It was as if they were in love and became children again, listening to stories and playing along. During our nine months together, all the grandmas and grandpas would look forward to our regular Tuesday visit. As for us, every visit was a blessing. Delicious food would be waiting, and there would be a lot to learn. We have to make this book to show how much we appreciate them.

T | Before this book, you were also making a play with elderly people.
E | Yes. This project was Tiny West's and Denny Cheng's idea. If I were initiating, I would have chosen visual art, but they chose drama right away. In the beginning, they used the form of playback theatre to enable people to recall their memories. Then, we used the historical background of Hong Kong and turned their stories into a play. Their stories might be ordinary, but they are all very valuable. Some of them are memories we also share, such as fleeing from the war and "dumping nocturnal fragrance". Some may seem somewhat unbelievable now. I remember a grandma saying she saw someone eating bamboo leaves to soothe his hunger. And then he died from it.

Our budget for this book is very limited. I am very grateful for the sponsorship from the Miramar Group. We also had the chance to perform the play and present an exhibition at the Hong Kong Heritage Museum. We have also been lucky to have many volunteers helping on the project. Esther was a volunteer, and then she helped with the props and part of the editing work for the recipes in this book.

T | Many people put their hearts into this project.
E | In every stage! One day I was on Peel Street, and I saw a curious looking Westerner with a very old camera strolling along. I went up to him and we started chatting. He loved food and I told him about this project. He then took the portraits of all these grandmas and grandpas. This man is Michael Wolf.

T | What is the most rewarding aspect about this project for you?
E | My cooking skills have improved! I have also gotton my taste buds back. Nowadays, we can buy as many readymade sauces and marinades as we want, but our sense of taste might still be numb. The elderly people always say we should make our own. Bean Paste Fish, for instance, needs the mixture of three kinds of pastes. This is for three reasons: to enrich the texture of the food, to marinade, and to give a good look to the dish. I follow their way of making it. I can really feel the difference from the tip of my tongue all the way to the back.

Also, the way they make sesame soup requires a kind of mashing stick. I can't find it anywhere in Hong Kong. And then I realized it was made from the wood of guava trees. When I went back to my hometown, I found a person who could make the stick. He made two for me. I took them back to the center and the grandmas and grandpas were so excited! They wanted

說沒有什麼回憶可言。

故事未完，尚留待其他人說說他們的故事……

to show me how to use it! It was like meeting an old friend who wanted to show off. I tried it myself. It wasn't easy at all. You have to hold the bowl in place by squeezing your thighs and then stir the stick in a firm but gentle way. The next week we went back, we were treated with sweet sesame soup.

Then another grandma said she knew how to make her own *lai fun* (a kind of glazy white noodles). Nowadays, lai fun is made from melting rice noodles. The texture is entirely lost. *Lai fun* should be made from rice kept for at least a day, mixed with rice noodles. They are then pressed out of punctuated iron plates. The more we talk with them, the more I find out about the lost tastes. It's like finding a part of me that has been lost.

T | Our traditional foodways carry values that are different from modern culture. I long for them. If they are lost forever, it would be a terrible waste.
E | Our everyday rhythm is too fast for anyone to handle. There is little time and space for us to sit down and reflect. There used to be less information, less distraction. Every dish could be made slowly, everything cut mindfully. Now, you watch TVB, then Cable TV, then CNN, BBC, CCTV-9...You get to know so many things. And yet this kind of information is very distant and unfamiliar. For me there isn't much of a memory about those things.

The story isn't over. It's time for others to speak...

他們就只有一個煲，一個爐灶，但能煮出出色的菜餚，
相比之下，西方的廚房，還要比一輛汽車貴。

與 MICHAEL WOLF 午間小敍

楊陽

再翻開 Tove Jansson 的 The Summer Book，是為了準備見 Michael。那是爭取保留天星碼頭行動的日子，正處於半睡半醒、半拉半扯、半明半不明的狀態，腦是「一舊雲」似的。加上對人家的名氣的慣性矛盾——三分一懷疑三分二盲目崇拜，決定找點事做，為「一舊雲」設個好好的場景，保持開揚廣闊。這場景，又怎可能不是夏天？

The Summer Book 發生在蒸氣沐浴的蔚藍天空下的小島。小島位於芬蘭海峽，小得只要四分半鐘就能圍繞一周。婆婆和小 Sophia在「四分半小島」度假，兩人在草叢石罅找婆婆掉了的假牙，理直氣壯地闖入鄰島，抗議鄰居的新房子破壞水平線的一望無際，在小島感受風暴，又和 Sophia 討論死亡，說愛情故事。

我從來沒想過這些安於度日的瑣事是脆弱的，我以為它們在時間的排序裡都活得安好。也許，這是我把自己放在安全距離的安好——是枯死的安好。就這樣，聖誕前幾天的一個中午，約了Michael在中環見面。這，卻是錯得離譜的。Michael主動告訴我，恨不得和家人逃離「案發現場」，什麼商場消費、節日沖喜都「無眼睇」。

然而，Michael 就是沒逃，反而一留就留了十二年。除了因為鏡頭看到更多，也是對味道的投降。十二年前，Michael因中國菜的色香味，毅然由加州移居香港。「當時，我腦子裡有個地球，我飛往亞爾巴尼亞，又到俄羅斯，但我不能去莫斯科，因為那裡只有伏特加和肥膩的大肉腸。」

相反，追隨中國菜的決定，來得像頓悟。說時，Michael像要向食得是福投降。這也同時是向能和身邊的人緊密接觸之福投降。「跟老人家一起，我感到舒暢，和祖母擁抱，對我來講是最自然不過的。」在德國杜塞爾多夫唸大學的時候，Michael 趁星期天學校休假時到祖母家探望。祖母為他準備一道簡單的菜：馬鈴薯伴麵包屑雞胸和肉腸。飯後他們一起散步。

為了這本書，Michael也嚐了很多老人家的拋手小菜。「每位老人家都有個秘密食譜，不好好紀錄的話，它們就會被遺忘。」Michael 特別記得把一個叫芝麻米糕的甜品帶回家，小兒 Jaspar 高興不已，要爸爸以後多弄。對 Michael 來說，食譜不僅是指南，更是老人家日常生活的點滴，也是生活豐盛的痕跡。「老人家活得比我開心，他們坐在走廊談天說地就過了豐富的大半天，我卻要很多才滿足。」

不久前，Michael 為了另一個老人家日常生活的攝影工作，到石硤尾多個公共屋苑探望多位八九十歲的老人家。Michael 清楚記得每家百呎單位內的細節。「每間房都有一個時鐘，一個日曆，一座電風扇和一個冰箱。」Michael 認為這些都是這城市的「文化建築」，也是他自身文化的寫照。「他們就只有一個煲，一個爐灶，但能煮出出色的菜餚，相比之下，西方的廚房，還要比一輛汽車貴。這又必定能煮好菜嗎？！」

AN AFTERNOON WITH MICHAEL WOLF

YEUNG YANG

Not long before I was to meet Michael, I treated myself to another reading of Tove Jansson's *The Summer Book*. At the time, I was preoccupied with the protests against the demolition of the old Star Ferry Pier and Clocktower. Those of us who were involved found ourselves torn between rage and resignation, lightness and weight, uncertainty and conviction, reality and abstraction. It didn't seem to be the best time for slow conversation with someone I'd never met, in a language I'd never felt so acutely foreign. The need to lean on some kind of simplicity where curiosity can breathe was urgent.

The Summer Book first caught my eye as I was browsing the shelves of a bookshop. The cover, with its little bushy island and big, bright blue sky, called to me. The book is about an elderly woman sharing her fears and desires with her granddaughter as they spend a summer on a small island in the Gulf of Finland. Nothing much more dramatic happens than, say, Grandma losing her false teeth and searching for them amid the lush vegetation. There's nothing sentimental either, other than little Sophia, whose mother has died, noticing the space left in the bed when her father wakes during the night to put another log on the fire. At one stage, Grandma takes a stand against a neighbour who has built a house with a "huge, angry, glittering [tin] roof". Not only does the house spoil the view, but the neighbour has had the temerity to erect a "No Trespassing" sign. "No well-bred person goes ashore on someone else's island when there's no one home," Grandma says. "But if they put up a sign, then you do it anyway, because it's a slap in the face."

I never used to think that little things—funny little everyday things—were a cause for concern. I thought they could mostly be ignored because they were safe. Now, I think this complacency comes from a desire to avoid getting close. Not getting close keeps you safe; but it's a dead kind of safety. Reading *The Summer Book* was the first time I have been deeply touched by an elderly person—her mischief, her honesty and her bluntness. And then came Michael. As he ran through the twists and turns of his childhood, I found myself immersed once again in the joy of getting close to an elderly person. There's a Chinese saying that living with an elderly person is like having a gem at home.

We met a little before Christmas. "I hate Christmas," Michael said. "I want to get away." The crowds, the shopping malls that all look the same, the frenzy of buying… Is this just Christmas, or Hong Kong in general, I wondered. And if Hong Kong is so disappointing, what drew him here in the first place? "Food," he said in a tone of surrender. "All the good memories I have are somehow related to food." Twelve years ago, Michael was living in California. "In my mind I had a globe," he said. "I started going to Albania, Russia… but I couldn't go to Moscow because there's only vodka and fatty sausages." And then suddenly the tastes and smells of Chinese food came into his mind and it clicked: Hong Kong. "Everything in my body said yes. It was an epiphany." But it wasn't just the tastes and smells of food. It was the human aspects of food that made Michael's decision such a happy one.

And what attracted him to this project? "I've been lucky," he said. "I feel very comfortable around elderly people. I have no problem hugging my grandmother,

隨緣

六十年代，十五歲的Michael走到加州街頭的民權示威，拍攝到穿著武裝的警察的照片，卻沒想過會成為職業攝影師。「那年我跟朋友出海，卻把帆船撞壞了，唯有折返，在家碰上爸爸的朋友，他是當年德國最有名唸攝影的大學的教授，他看畢我拍的照片，就鼓勵我申請報讀交換生計劃。我當時在加州柏克萊大學唸書，四個月後，我就被接納了。」大學是一所舊修道院，很大的窗，很廣闊的花園。不久，Michael就知道當攝影記者是賺錢的，就拿著論文，到漢堡和曼徹斯特工作。

説起現在的生活，Michael又自然談起食的故事。除了來自斯里蘭卡的家庭傭工用的特製香料外，還有這本書的來由。「第一次遇到二胡婆婆時，我正在卑利街拍照。二胡婆婆說我的攝影機像是上世紀的古董。我說那只是六十年代的產物。就這樣，我們開始談天説地，談大牌檔、街市、餃子……」我想，一天我們忘掉食的故事，也是我們抹掉親密經驗的時候。

禮物

翻譯這些故事的時候，我想起以前照顧我和三個姐姐的家傭「豬寬」(我們為她起的花名)。豬寬像本書的幾位婆婆一樣，是順德人，年青時已決定梳起不嫁。我沒有問過豬寬原因。後來我想，問她會令她尷尬。其實尷尬的是自己——那時覺得結婚是必然的，不結婚必定是出了「問題」。

豬寬能煮簡單又好味的時令菜。冬天，豬寬煮「狗仔」，即甜湯泡麵粉條，有時就吃油鹽雞蛋飯。冷冰冰的早上，上學前拿著熱騰騰的飯碗食一頓，暖透心! 過年，豬寬就弄炸芋蝦。這食品就像一小堆棉絲，又輕又脆。我特別愛它叫芋蝦，好像芋頭如蝦在跳。夏天，我們就吃禮拜六特別餐——蛋絲冬菇荷蘭豆炒銀針粉。這簡直是自由的象徵，因為這是爸媽不在家才有的美食。

也因為豬寬煮不同的食物，我慢慢體會到爸媽的階級教育。豬寬喜歡在飯面蒸豆腐卜或鹹魚，但我們從來不會在飯桌吃這些，豬寬只會一個人在廚房吃她的，我們在飯廳吃我們的。有時候，家裡只有我們倆，我就往廚房跟她坐著紅A膠凳吃飯。很久以後我才知道這是爸媽不想我超越的社會界線。不過，豬寬退休後到公共屋邨住，媽媽竟然不時和我一起去看她。

豬寬和其他老人家的故事不單是有血有肉的歷史，也紀錄了他們面對戰亂、窮困等逆境的種種。老人家有自己說自由、行自由的法子；自由並不是年青人的專利。

不肯定應否稱Michael「伯伯」，不知道他的反應會怎樣。但跟他接觸，讓我感到一種只有公公婆婆才有的鬼馬，是一種能遠達無形，靜悄悄看守著庸俗的鬼馬。可學，可重學的，還多的是。

for instance." Michael fondly remembers visiting his grandmother every Sunday morning in Düsseldorf during university holidays. She would cook him simple food: chicken breast in bread crumbs with lemon juice, along with sausages and potatoes. After the meals, they would take a walk together.

For this project, Michael visited many elderly people and went to cooking parties. "Every elderly person has a secret recipe," he said. "And if you don't write it down, it will be gone forever." There's one delicacy Michael remembers in particular: a rice-based jelly dessert with black sesame. He brought some home and his son, Jaspar, loved it so much he kept asking for more. For Michael, the recipes in this book aren't merely instructions for preparing subsistence food—they're tangible memories of bountiful and beautiful lives. "I need a lot to be satisfied," he said. "But the elderly people are so happy. They sit in corridors, talking about food and telling stories to each other." These recipes are inextricably tied up with the elderly—their homes, their lives and their past. Michael recalls meeting grandmothers and grandfathers in their eighties and nineties living in apartments of no more than about one hundred square feet. "Each room has a clock, a calendar, a fan and a fridge," he said. "They have one pot, one flame, but their food still tastes really good. Think of the Western kitchen, with gear that costs as much as a car." Michael said he particularly enjoys projects like this because they make the elderly people feel needed. "Everyone has a story and each story has a value. This is how family history is passed on. Old people tell their grandchildren what it was like in the old days. Their memories are invaluable."

No surprise, then, that it was food that brought Michael and Auntie Evelyna together—a relationship that would eventually give rise to the book you're now reading. "I was taking some photographs on Peel Street. Evelyna came over and asked me about my camera, which she said looked like it was from the last century. In fact, I'd had it since the sixties. We started chatting about *dai pai dongs* and markets." When it comes to food, Michael's mind is full of marvellous memories of serendipities and human touches. If we lose the memories associated with food, I thought, we lose a vital touchstone of intimate experiences.

As I was translating the stories in this book, I remembered my nanny, who took care of me and my sisters, and the food she used to make for us and for herself. We called her Piggy Foon, although she was very thin. Foon was her first name, which means many things, including "forgiveness" (寬恕) in Chinese.

She often made us sweet "puppy congee" for breakfast in winter. It's simply shredded flour in a clear, hot sweet soup. Sometimes, Piggy Foon would splash beaten eggs onto rice when it was almost cooked, then add a little oil and sprinkle on salt. Holding a bowl of this rice full to the brim during the winter was such a treat! At Chinese New Year, Piggy Foon would make us snacks of deep-fried shredded taro. They looked like small bundles of wool, only they were crispy and light. The Chinese name means "taro shrimp" and as a child I loved the idea of taro hopping and swimming like shrimp. In the summer, we had special Saturday lunches of fried silver needle noodles with egg, Chinese mushrooms and Holland beans. It wasn't only a wonderful break from routine meals, but even now I still associate it with a sense of freedom—because we had these noodles only when mum and dad were out, leaving me and my sisters at home to do as we pleased.

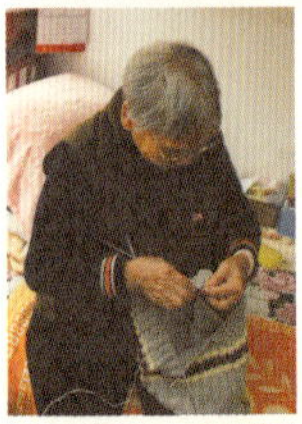

EVERY ELDERLY PERSON HAS A SECRET RECIPE. IF YOU DON'T WRITE IT DOWN, IT WILL BE GONE FOREVER.

Piggy Foon didn't eat with us, and the food she made for herself was different from what we ate in the dining room. I remember thinking Piggy Foon ate in the kitchen because she liked it there. One day, when only she and I were at home, I ate with her there, sitting on a Red A brand plastic stool. Only much later did I realise that there was a social division between us that my parents didn't want me to cross.

Piggy Foon was from Shun De—a place known as the home of many young women who decide to "tie up their hair" and remain single. I never asked Piggy Foon how or why she made that decision—even after she had retired and I would sometimes visit her at the housing estate where she lived with her sister. And now I will never know. I used to justify to myself that she would have been embarrassed if I'd asked her about it. But, of course, it would have been me who'd have felt embarrassed—me, who always thought marriage was so important for a woman. Piggy Foon's stories and the many others collected here aren't only social histories, but also a documentation of individual spirit. The elderly have their own ways of being free. True freedom is not the privilege of the young.

I have referred to Michael here as an elderly person. I don't know how he will react. Given the high regard he has for the elderly, I hope he will take it as a compliment. One thing is certain, though. He has allowed us to see and sense, through his work and words, the special mischief of which only grandmas and grandpas are capable—that quiet quality of feeling their way through to that which doesn't belong to the worldly, because it's behind or beyond its time. There is so much to learn and unlearn.

目錄 Index

婆婆女書 I Am

邊做邊學 I Learn

回味 I Taste

情
LOVE

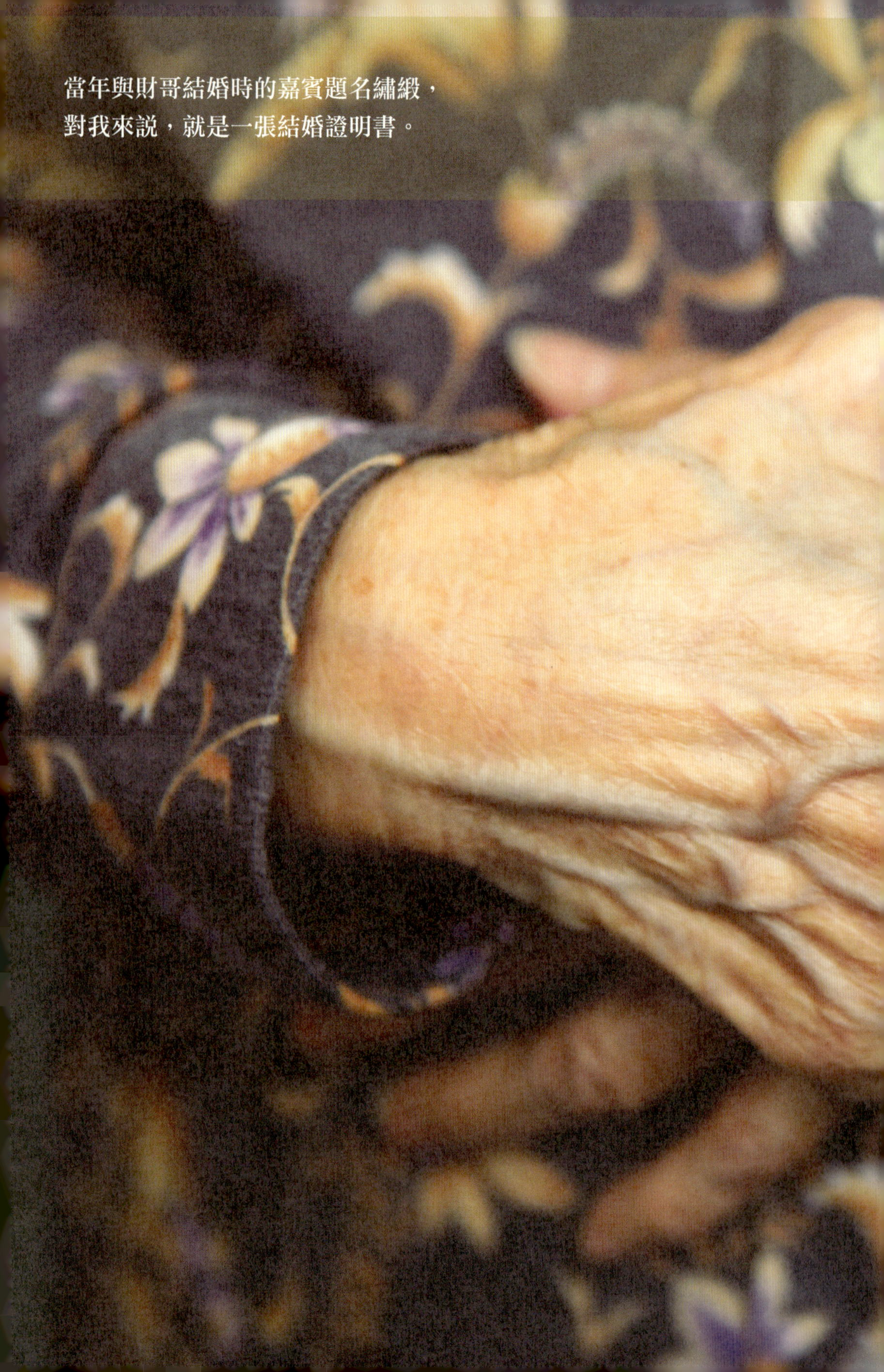

當年與財哥結婚時的嘉賓題名繡緞，
對我來說，就是一張結婚證明書。

My workmates at the garment factory
made a beautiful embroidery for me
with the names of all our wedding guests on it.
For me, that embroidery is my marriage certificate.

陳賀春　七十九歲　祖籍南海西樵

噢！我差點兒忘了自己是哪一年出生的，好像是1961年，不，是1931年？就這樣，義工都愛叫我「阿春」、「阿春」的。那天，義工叮囑我帶珍藏來給他們拍照，我帶了一張當年與財哥結婚時的嘉賓題名繡緞，那是我們一起在製衣廠工作時，一班工友親手給我們繡的。那時候沒有到婚姻註冊處註冊，只是一班親友吃一頓飯，擺過喜酒然後洞房罷了。這一張繡緞現在對我來說，就是一張結婚證明書。提起繡緞，記得幼年時，我就常常坐在母親身旁，邊看她給人家繡花，邊聽她給我唸《三字經》。我就是這樣慢慢的聽著、學著。母親去世時我才八歲，及後跟父親和後母來港，沒有機會讀書，十多歲就學車衣。常與一班工友一起逛街看電影。每次假期，我最期待的節目就是看戲。那時我們會一起由青山道走到旺角的新華戲院看電影。印象最深刻的影片是《一江春水向東流》。在親戚安排下認識了同廠工作的財哥，廿一歲結婚，之後兒女相繼出生，我在製衣廠工作直到退休。孩子上學讀書，我就在旁伴讀，文字就是這樣學懂了。後來，更跟女兒到教會，讀聖經、唱詩歌……現在我的文化水平還頂高呢！記起童年時愛吃的東西是那七彩斑斕的禾蟲。看著那些東西蠕動的確有點可怕，不過煮熟後卻是如此好看又好味。現在想吃也吃不到了！我最拿手的小菜是番茄煮紅衫魚，紅紅的，蠻好看。與其說這是我最愛弄的一道菜，不如說是女兒最愛吃的一味吧！甜甜酸酸，有蔬果，有魚肉，更有豐富的營養呢。我煮的魚是不會有腥味的！

看電影是當時十分普遍的娛樂，甚至好些地方在同一條街道就有兩三間戲院。戲院外會有各式小吃攤檔，如燒魷魚或粟米，又香又熱鬧。而《一江春水向東流》是50年代著名導演蔡楚生和鄭君里合作的電影，有謂是中國電影史上第一部「史詩式影片」。

When I was very young, I used to sit next to my mother and watch her make embroidered flowers. While she was working, she would read to me the *San Zi Jing*, a text book for primary students composed of three-character phrases. I listened and slowly learned. My mother died when I was eight. After my father remarried, we moved to Hong Kong. I never

had the chance to study again. When I was about ten, I started work at a factory using a sewing machine. After work, we used to stroll the streets. Sometimes we would walk all the way from Castle Peak Road to the Sun Wah Cinema in Mongkok. I remember one film particularly well: Spring River Flowing Towards the East.

This film was made in the 1950s. It was later known as the first epic film in Chinese film history.

Eventually, a relative introduced me to my future husband, who also worked in the factory. We got married when I was twenty-one, although we didn't go to the marriage registry. We had dinner with our relatives and friends, and that was regarded as the wedding banquet and our "first night". My workmates at the garment factory made a beautiful embroidery for me with the names of all our wedding guests on it. For me, that embroidery is my marriage certificate. I started having children when I was twenty-five. When my children went to school, I would sometimes go with them. That's how I learned to read and write. Later, I went with my daughter to church. I learned the Bible and sang hymns. When I was small, I loved to eat grain worms. It was a bit scary watching them wriggle in the water. But once they were cooked, they looked nice and tasted wonderful. I still make red mullet with tomatoes, which also looks good. I don't especially like making it, but my daughter loves to eat it. It's sweet and sour and is very nutritious.

Dace Balls with Chinese Lettuce in Casserole

250 g dace fillet
1 large piece dried tangerine peel
few dried shrimps
2 pieces bean curd
2 stalks Chinese lettuce
6 cups clear broth
some sliced ginger and minced garlic
marinade : 1 tsp cornstarch, some pepper, 1 tbsp cooked water

1 Finely chop dace fillet until sticky. Set aside.
2 Soak dried shrimps until soft; chop finely. Soak dried tangerine peel until soft. Scrape off pith and cut into fine dices. Set aside.
3 Rinse Chinese lettuce and cut into small portions. Set aside.
4 In a big round bowl, add seasoning, dried shrimp and tangerine peel into the dace flesh.
5 Mix and stir in one direction until sticky.
6 Shape fish meat into one big ball.
7 Slap the dace flesh back and forth against the side of a big bowl 10-20 times*.
8 Add in ginger slices and minced garlic when clear broth boils.
9 Shape fish flesh into fish balls with a spoon. Put fish balls into broth and keep boiling until they float.
10 Lastly, add in bean curd and Chinese lettuce.
11 Bring all ingredients to a boil. Add seasonings according to individual taste.

** Slapping the dace flesh with force against the side of a big bowl makes the fish ball bouncy in texture.*

To make the dish more wholesome, add winter mushrooms.

鯪魚球生菜豆腐煲

鯪魚肉250克
果皮1大塊
蝦米少量
豆腐2塊
唐生菜2棵
上湯6碗
薑片及蒜蓉各適量
醃料：生粉1茶匙、胡椒粉適量及凍滾水1湯匙

1 鯪魚肉剁碎，備用
2 果皮和蝦米浸軟後剁蓉，備用
3 唐生菜摘開，備用
4 於大圓碗內，將鯪魚肉加入醃料，再加入果皮和蝦米蓉
5 混合後，以同一方向將所有材料攪成膠狀
6 用手將魚膠滾成球狀
7 將魚膠往碗邊撻10-20次*，備用
8 上湯煲滾後加入薑片和蒜蓉
9 用茶匙將魚膠做成球狀，放進上湯內滾至浮起
10 加入豆腐和唐生菜
11 所有材料煲滾後，按個人口味作適量調味

* 將魚膠往碗邊大力撻，能使魚肉更爽滑彈牙。撻魚膠時可先抹少許油在手心，那麼魚肉便不會黏手

加入冬菇，令這道菜更健康有益

只見數艘「躉船」一字排列，
這就是擺設數十席「愛筵」的地方。

There would be several barges lined up in a row.
Dozens of tables would be set up.
What a scene—so jolly and boisterous!

黎慧珍　八十三歲　祖籍東莞

自從出世後，我便與海結下不解之緣。我是否「蜑家人」？那就不太清楚，不過，有一點我是可以肯定的，兒時及婚前的居所是一艘船，那麼我就是「水上人」吧！結婚後，我便搬往旺角一幢戰前樓宇中居住。不說你不知，那時每晚都飄來陣陣的「夜來香」，因為沒有抽水馬桶，有人就提供收集糞便的「倒夜香」服務，所以「夜來香」自是「倒夜香」所帶來的惡臭。話說回來，吃喜酒的時候，可真是壯觀非常！首先由家中，走路往油麻地避風塘，然後乘搭「水上的士」，即人手搖櫓的那一種接駁小艇。搖呀！搖呀！搖！跟著泊近一艘船。放眼一望，只見數艘「躉船」一字排列，這就是擺設數十席「愛筵」的地方。場面可偉大，熱鬧非常！不論親戚、朋友、大人或小朋友，都可以在那些躉船之間來去自如，如履平地，吃喝玩樂，不亦樂乎！生離死別，誰可避免？對於我的宗族來說，喪禮上也有一些特別的儀式，那就是唱哀歌，如山歌般清唱的「哀歌」，不是對唱，是個人獨唱，歌詞及內容，是個人對逝去親人的哀傷表達。你問我怎樣唱？我也不太懂得，在同輩中，現在碩果僅存，只有一人懂得唱。相信年輕的一代，如我的兒女，他們對此儀式的深層意義也未曾認識，更遑論秉承傳統了！記得六十年代住板間房時，自己要外出工作，母親在家協助打理家務。由於居住環境十分狹小，母親又愛烹飪，所以每當做糯米釀大腸時，都要將碌架床下層之床板掤開，才能騰出空間，讓祖孫三代合力完成菜式。雖然看似勞師動眾，但為我們帶來了一個既可玩耍，又可飽餐一頓的機會。如今，我的孫兒及孫女大多數都學業有成，投身社會了。最近，兒女如獲至寶地告訴我，「水上人」喜歡坐「凳仔」的生活文化，仍能在他們身上找到一鱗半爪。哈！哈！意想不到！意想不到！

早年大量移民來港，不少業主將單位分隔多個房間出租或讓親屬暫居。每房間通常約一百平方呎，可放置一張床及一個雜物櫃，由於房與房只是一（木）板之隔，往往可聽到鄰室之聲，同單位的不同房戶又自有其鄰舍關係。若住客的經濟能力有改善，便會搬離。現多是低收入人士的居所。

Ever since I was born, I've felt close to the sea. I don't know if my ethnic origin is Tanka, but I lived on a boat until I got married, so I think I can be considered a person "living on the water". Sometimes, there would be spectacular banquets! We would walk from home to the typhoon shelter in Yau Ma Tei. Then we'd take a "water taxi", which was just

a boat rowed by one person. There would be several barges lined up in a row. Dozens of tables would be set up. What a scene—so jolly and boisterous! There would be relatives and friends, adults and children. It was such fun. However, with the joy of life comes the pain of life. Who can escape from parting and death? There's a ritual my clan practices at a funeral called "singing the sad songs". They're always sung solo, without musical accompaniment. The lyrics express the pain of losing a relative. I don't really know how to sing them. It would be difficult to find anyone who knows them now. There's only one person I know who can do it. The younger generation don't understand the deeper meanings of such a ritual, let alone those of other traditions. I remember during the 1960s, when we lived in make-shift rooms with wooden boards for walls, I had to work and so my mother would help with the household chores. The space was very small, but my mother loved to cook. Whenever she made sausage stuffed with glutinous rice, we had to take away the boards of the lower deck of the two-tiered bed to make some space. All of us from three generations helped to make the dish. It gave us a chance to play and eat together.

It was common in those days that landlords divided apartments with wooden boards into make-shift rooms of 100 square feet each to rent them out to people with a low income.

糖環

麵粉、粟粉、鮮奶各120克
雞蛋4隻
糖、椰漿各180克
水240克
糖環模具1-2個

1 將糖、椰漿、鮮奶、水放進深碗中，並打入雞蛋，拌勻
2 麵粉、粟粉同篩勻，然後加入蛋混合液內，攪拌成粉漿，備用
3 用粉篩過濾已調好的粉漿
4 將糖環模具放中式鑊中，與油一同燒熱，提起模具，讓多餘的油滴回鑊中
5 立刻把模具放入粉漿內，讓粉漿沾在上面，但不可浸過模面
6 隨即把模具放到熱油中，炸至粉漿自動脫離模具，並呈金黃色

須注意油的溫度。
亦須注意模具的溫度，不夠熱無法上粉，太熱則粉漿過早脫離模具

Sugar Ring

120g each flour, corn flour and fresh milk
4 eggs
180 g sugar and coconut paste
240 g water
1 to 2 sugar ring moulds

1 Put sugar, coconut paste, fresh milk and water in a deep bowl. Whisk in egg and mix.
2 Sift flour and corn flour. Add in egg mixture to make a flour paste. Set aside.
3 Strain flour paste with flour sift to make it smooth.
4 Put sugar ring mould into a Chinese wok and heat with oil. Remove mould and drip excess oil into wok.
5 Immediately dip mould into flour paste so that the paste sticks into the mould but make sure its top surface is clear of the paste.
6 Put mould into hot oil and fry until the paste turns golden yellow and detaches from mould automatically.

Pay attention to the temperature of oil when deep-frying.
Make sure the sugar ring mould is heated at the right temperature—if it is not hot enough, the paste cannot stick on; if it's too hot, the paste will detach from the mould too quickly.

香糯鳳翼

雞中翼12隻
冬菇6隻（切絲）
紅蘿蔔1/4個（切片）
上湯約170克
薑蓉、蔥粒、乾蔥蓉、蒜蓉各1湯匙
醃料：豉油3湯匙，糖、鹽各1/2茶匙，胡椒粉少許，紹興酒1湯匙，粟粉1茶匙
餡料：糯米1/2杯，花生1湯匙（浸5小時後去衣剁碎），蝦米1湯匙（浸軟切粒），榨菜粒1湯匙
調味：鹽、糖、蠔油、粟粉各少許

1 雞翼洗淨，瀝乾水分，去骨，然後下醃料，醃約30分鐘
2 糯米洗淨，用水浸5小時後，瀝乾水分，與其他餡料拌勻放深碗中，隔水蒸熟，待冷備用
3 將已蒸熟的餡料釀入醃好的雞翼內，只需釀半滿，然後走油
4 燒熱鍋，下油，爆香薑蓉、乾蔥蓉、蒜蓉、冬菇絲、紅蘿蔔片
5 加入雞翼、上湯*、調味料，滾後慢火煮10分鐘，用粟粉開水勾芡，灑上蔥粒便可

* 浸冬菇水可代替上湯

鳴謝：嚴婉芬女士提供烹調方法

Stuffed Chicken Wing with Flavoured Glutinous Rice

12 pieces mid-joint chicken wings
6 pieces winter mushroom, shredded
¼ stalk carrot, sliced
170 g clear broth
1 tbsp each ginger, spring onion, shallot and garlic, finely chopped
marinade : 3 tbsp soy sauce, ½ tsp each sugar and salt, some pepper, 1 tbsp Shaoxing wine, 1 tsp cornstarch
fillings : ½ cup flavoured glutinous rice; 2 pieces mushroom, soaked and diced; 1 tbsp peanut, soaked for 5 hours, de-skinned and finely chopped; 1 tbsp dried shrimp, soaked and diced; 1 tbsp preserved mustard cabbage
seasoning : some salt, sugar, oyster sauce and cornstarch

1 Rinse chicken wings, drip-dry. De-bone and marinade for about 30 minutes.
2 Wash glutinous rice and soak for 5 hours. Let dry, mix with fillings. Place in deep bowl, steam until cooked. Set aside and let cool.
3 Stuff (half full) the cooked fillings into the marinaded chicken wings and shallow fry.
4 Heat wok with oil. Stir fry all ingredients except chicken wings.
5 When flavour smells, add in chicken wings, clear broth*, and seasonings. When boiled, reset to low heat and cook for 10 minutes. Lastly, add cornstarch water and fry together briefly. Sprinkle chopped spring onion and serve.

* *Water from soaked mushroom is another substitute for clear broth.*

Many thanks to Ms Yim Yuen Fun for the recipe.

拜堂時，低著頭，
才僅僅在蒙面的蓋頭下
見到丈夫拿著拜堂酒杯的手。

I kept my head down.
That was when I got my first glimpse
of my future husband holding a wine glass.

梁桂芳　八十一歲　祖籍南海

我當然是「順得」人。七、八歲左右就經常幫母親照顧弟妹。十二歲慶幸有機會入學讀書。兒時沒有什麼吃喝玩樂，在鄉下種到什麼就吃什麼，沒有特別要求！玩耍嘛……也沒有玩什麼的，姊妹們叫我做什麼，我就做什麼啦！別人對我一切的安排，我都會默默接受，連婚事也一樣。丈夫的樣子是怎樣的，我婚前也不知道，很聽話就出嫁啦。出嫁前我還要待在家中好幾天不准出外。到大轎抬我去拜堂時，跪在大圓筲箕上，低著頭，才僅僅在蒙面的蓋頭下見到丈夫拿著拜堂酒杯的手，才算第一次接觸到他。我作媳婦後的一個月才敢抬頭看丈夫的樣貌，當時心中可又驚又怕！十五歲半拜堂，十七歲還差兩個月就生了第一個孩子。丈夫和我的感情很好，我們雖然說話不多，但因為我讀過書，他什麼事都會讓我處理。我從不用為自己求什麼。年少時喜歡吃的是豆角焗魚或焗豬肉，現時最希望能吃到的是【芋頭焗魚】。放點麵豉，可又濕又香。今天已很少吃得到了，因現在我不用煮飯，家中一切都交給媳婦處理，我樂得清閒。她們愛煮什麼，我就吃什麼囉。也許我最愛吃的是雞翼尖吧！慢慢細嚼，美味就從皮滲到肉滲到骨呢。

中國傳統婚禮儀式，亦稱「拜天地」。新郎新娘均衣著鮮紅，以示喜慶。新娘另戴鳳冠面紗，有拜堂不見臉之禮。拜堂前燃燭焚香、鳴爆竹奏樂，然後新郎新娘就位跪拜，一拜天地，二拜父母，三夫妻對拜。返回房間，新郎才掀起新娘之蓋頭。

I'm definitely a *Shun Tak Yan*. [*Shun Tak* is a city in Guangdong, which puns with "easy-going"; *Yan* means person.] When I was seven or eight, I started helping my mother take care of my brother and sister. We ate what we grew and didn't need much. We didn't have much to play with. I usually did whatever my sisters told me to do! When I was twelve, I was lucky

enough to be able to go to school. I always followed what other people arranged for me—even my marriage. I didn't even know what my future husband looked like before we got married. I was very obedient. Before the wedding, I had to stay home for several days. Then, they brought me on a sedan chair to the *bai tang* ceremony and I knelt on a round rattan mat. I kept my head down. That was when I got my first glimpse of my future husband holding a wine glass. A month later we got married and I finally got a good look at his face. I was so scared! I was fifteen-and-a-half when I got married. Two months before I turned seventeen, I gave birth to my first child. My husband and I got along very well. We didn't talk much, but because I'd been to school, he let me handle things. I used to like braised beans with fish or pork. Now, I like Braised Taro with Fish. Adding soya bean paste makes it juicy and aromatic. These days, I let my daughter-in-law handle everything at home. I'm happy to be free. I eat whatever she makes. I like the tips of chicken wings. I slowly chew on them and enjoy the taste in the bones.

Bai tang, or bowing to the altar, is also known as *bai tian di*, or bowing to the sky and earth. The bride wears a veil, and the groom cannot look into her face until they have bowed to the sky and earth, to their parents, and to each other.

芋頭燜魚

石斑魚腩／龍脷魚柳450克
芋頭半個
薑數片
蒜粒2瓣
蔥花少量
蔥段數段
豆粉及紹興酒各1湯匙
指天椒1隻
水半杯

1 芋頭刨去厚皮，切成長方形厚片，放入燒紅之油鑊，用中火炸至金黃色，取出隔油，備用
2 魚腩切厚片，用薑、蔥、蒜起鑊，慢火煎香兩面，備用
3 於瓦鍋中放進上湯、水半杯、薑2片、蔥段，滾開
4 下芋頭，煮至半腍後下魚塊*
5 以慢火燜至收水
6 上碟後以蔥花伴碟

* 好辣者可放指天椒跟芋頭和魚同燜

Braised Taro with Fish

450 g garoupa belly / snapper fillet
½ kg taro
ginger few slices
2 cloves garlic
some chopped spring onions
few stalks of sectioned spring onions
1 tbsp corn starch
1 tbsp Shaoxing wine
1 chilli
½ cup water

1 Peel taro, cut into long thick slices. Deep-fry in wok with heated oil until golden yellow. Remove and drain oil. Set aside.
2 Cut fish belly into thick slices. In a heated wok, sauté ginger, spring onions and garlic with oil. Add wine. Reset to low heat and fry both sides of fish belly until fragrant. Set aside.
3 In a casserole dish, put ½ cup of water, 2 slices of ginger, chilli and the sectioned spring onions. Bring to a boil.
4 Add taro and cook until half-soft. Add fish belly slices*.
5 Braise on low heat until sauce thickens.
6 Garnish with chopped spring onions.

**For those who like spicy food, braise the taro and fish with chilli.*

第一次吃蜜餞雞時，還有妹仔服侍著吃呢！

When I used to cook for everyone at home,
I would buy four chickens—that's eight wings for the four of us.
Sometimes, we would fight over them!

李浩然 七十三歲 祖籍新會

我家族是廣東新會附近聞名的老饕，所以家中成員都蠻挑嘴，少時不曉得鮑參翅肚是什麼，只知不愛吃那些黑麻麻的……應該是海參吧！最愛吃那些一條條像牙籤的……應該是魚翅吧！阿姨和照顧我的人都說我年幼是非常頑皮的。父母生了幾個女兒後，以為不會有兒子了，怎知後來生下我，從此一家人便將我寵壞。他們叫我「阿妹」，因怕我養不大！在家裡，我差不多有求必應，每個人都聽我的，不敢得罪我。有一次，我不小心把一隻碗跌在地上，砰的一聲，我覺得很有趣，便笑起來了。家人見到那個情景，便把十幾隻碗都扔到地上，弄得砰砰啪啪的。為的，只是想逗我一笑。我八歲，第一次吃蜜餞雞，和十分疼惜我的外公一起吃，還有妹仔服侍著吃呢！那已是四九年解放前，母親親手為我們做的美食。當時孩子吃厭了雞肉，母親就施展出嫁前學來的私房菜，特地為我們弄這道有趣的甜膩菜式。多年以後，我已是家中出色的大廚，堅持用瓦煲煮飯。我最拿手的菜式，也是太太與孩子最愛的還是這一味——【甜甜蜜蜜比翼雙飛】。倒是自己弄來弄去，總沒有母親當年親手煮的好吃。煮雞翼的秘訣是要先用薑汁酒醃好，在爆熟時加入蜜糖慢火焗才入味，火候的掌握至為重要。雞翼一定要買新鮮的，這十分要緊。平常在家一煮就買四隻雞，總共有八隻翼，一家四口分吃剛剛好，但有時還是會爭吃哩！太太說起婚後初嚐此美味的雞翼，感覺是從來沒有吃過如此好吃的東西！自從兩個孩子往澳洲升學後，我就再沒有弄這味蜜餞雞翼了。

海參被稱為「大海之珍」，中國傳統名貴食材之一。海參本為吸吃海中浮游生物的棘皮類動物，醃製後可曬成乾貨。其肉質細嫩、富有彈性、鮮味爽口，是一種高蛋白低脂肪的營養食材，且有補腎經、益精髓、消痰涎、壯陽療萎、補髓生血等復元滋補之效。

Sea cucumber is known as "treasure of the sea" in Chinese cuisine. It can be sun-dried. It has a fine texture and is high in protein. It is good for the kidneys and spine.

My family are well-known food-lovers from Xinhui, in Guangdong. That's why all of us are very particular about our food. When I was young, I didn't know what abalone or shark's fin were. I only knew I liked to eat the black stuff. It was probably sea cucumber. And I loved the little "toothpicks" which were probably shark's fin. My aunt and those who took care

of me said I was very naughty. My parents had a few daughters before me and thought they would never get a son. So, when I was born they spoiled me. They called me *Ah Mui* [little sister] even though I was a boy because they were afraid I would never make it to adulthood. I always got what I wanted. Everyone always listened to what I said and tried never to upset me. I remember once dropping a bowl on the floor. I thought it was so funny that I started laughing. My family saw that and they started throwing bowls on the floor just to make me laugh. I was eight when I had honey-glazed chicken for the first time. I had it with my grandfather, who loved me a lot. This was before the liberation. My mother also made lovely food. Eventually, I became an outstanding chef. I always cook rice using the traditional sandy pot, but my prize dish—and the one my wife and children love best—is Sweet Honey Paired Chicken Wings. Even so, mine is no match for my mother's. The trick is to marinate the chicken wings with ginger wine and to cook them on a low heat. This ensures that they take in the flavour. It's also important to use fresh chicken wings. When I used to cook for everyone at home, I would buy four chickens—that's eight wings for the four of us. Sometimes, we would fight over them! My wife says that when I cooked this for her for the first time after we got married, she'd never tasted anything like it. Now that our two children have gone to study in Australia, I've stopped making it.

Li Ho Yin 73 years old Hometown Xinhui

甜甜蜜蜜比翼雙飛

雞中翼4隻
薑2片
蜜糖隨意
醃料：薑汁、玫瑰露酒各1茶匙，糖、粟粉各1/2茶匙，鹽適量，胡椒粉少許

1 雞翼洗淨，瀝乾水分
2 下醃料，醃約20分鐘
3 下油起鑊，爆香薑片*
4 放入雞翼爆至差不多熟透時，加入蜜糖
5 改用細火，煮至全熟即可食用

* 可選用子薑，味道清甜

Sweet Honey Paired Chicken Wings

4 mid-joint chicken wings
2 slices ginger*
some honey
marinade : 1 tsp ginger extract,
1 tsp Chinese rosé wine, ½ tsp sugar,
½ tsp cornstarch, some salt, few pinches pepper

1 Rinse chicken wings. Wipe dry.
2 Marinate for about 20 minutes.
3 Heat oil in wok. Stir-fry ginger slices.
4 Put in chicken wings and keep stir-frying until almost cooked. Add honey.
5 Reset to low heat. Cook until done. Remove from heat and serve.

** Use baby ginger for a sweet, fresh flavour*

郭素英　六十三歲　祖籍潮陽

我是家中長女，四、五歲隨家人來港定居，自小就要擔當大姐姐的角色，替父母照顧兩個弟弟和三個妹妹。後來為了幫補家計，十二三歲開始到塑膠廠工作做包裝。在工廠中認識了丈夫，他是廠長老闆的弟弟，在廠裡任職總管。有一年的三八婦女節，放工後，兩口子一路上談天說地，不經不覺由石塘咀行至今天香港大學附近的寶翠園。走累了，我們兩人便在路旁的樹下休息。他拿出特意到金唐餐廳買的幾個「椰撻」，教我驚喜不已，因為當時甚少機會吃點心，那次可是我第一次吃椰撻，那股香氣……我們相識了六年才結婚，婚後育有一子四女，子女不但孝順，學業成績亦相當優秀。每年的團年飯，我都會煮上多款菜式，當中又以薑片、黃糖炆，像被糖漿包裹的【黃糖芋頭】最受歡迎。

椰撻和蛋撻為南方特色甜點。椰撻參照蛋撻脆皮中以蛋黃烤成的製法，改於脆皮內放入椰絲，加少許蛋粉烘焙而成。

Kwok So Ying　63 year old　Hometown Chaoyang

I'm the oldest child in my family. We came to Hong Kong from the Mainland when I was about four or five. I always helped my parents take care of my younger brothers and sisters. When I was twelve, I started working in a plastic-packaging factory to contribute to the family income. I met my future husband in the factory. He was the chief manager and the brother of the owner. After we finished work one day—it was March 8, International Women's Day—we walked from Shek Tong Tsui, heading to where The Belcher's is now, near the University of Hong Kong. After a while, we got tired and rested under a tree. He took out a few coconut tarts, which he had bought from the Kam Tong Restaurant. I rarely got the chance to eat dim sum, and it was the first time I'd had a coconut tart. The aroma! About six years later, we got married. We have one son and four daughters. They were obedient and did very well at school. Every Chinese New Year, I still make all sorts of dishes. Taro in Ginger and Brown Sugar is the most popular in my family.

Coconut tarts and egg tarts are popular desserts in Southern China. Rather than using egg yolks, coconut tarts are made with shredded coconut and custard.

黃糖芋頭

芋頭半個（小）
薑片4片
黃糖2片（搗碎）
水適量

1 將芋頭切塊
2 熱鑊下油，炒香薑片後，加入芋頭*
3 芋頭炒至微黃時加入搗碎的黃糖，拌勻
4 加入水，加蓋燜至芋頭腍軟即成

* 可放蔥花、蒜蓉及少許鹽與芋頭同炒，有鹹香及甜之混合味道

Taro in Ginger and Brown Sugar

½ taro (small)
4 slices ginger
2 pieces of crushed brown sugar
some water

1 Cut taro into thick slices.
2 Pour oil into heated wok. Sauté ginger slices until fragrant, then add taro*.
3 Stir-fry taro until light yellow. Add crushed brown sugar. Mix well.
4 Add water. Cover and stew until taro slices turn soft. Serve.

** Frying the taro with chopped spring onions, minced garlic and a little salt gives the dish a sweet and salty taste.*

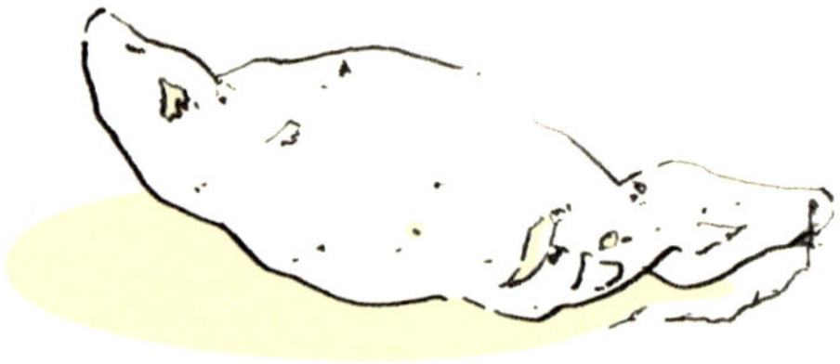

苦日子
BITTER DAYS

窗外，警察在放煙霧彈。
恐怖。我整天都不敢出外。

The police were throwing smoke bombs out on the streets.
It was horrifying.

窗外，警察在放煙霧彈。恐怖。我整天都不敢出外，一家人就躲在屋裡。那是「六七暴動」。我今年七十多歲了，那幾天的爆炸聲，至今記憶猶新，尚有些餘悸。我是五十年代來港定居的，童年時在鄉下居住。在鄉下，我年紀很小便開始工作，一家是當小販的，我就負責買賣食品，有時候也要下田幫手耕作，種菜、施肥、除雜草。空餘時間，不像現在的孩子，童年時並沒有什麼特別的玩具，多是跳繩，踢毽子，盪鞦韆。最喜歡的，就是打籃球。讀書時期，我差不多每天都打籃球呢。可惜家貧，小學未完成便要輟學。沒辦法，無錢，但一有機會還是會去上夜學。我的丈夫是由父母介紹的，當時他是做藥材的，在鄉下兩人一起長大，感情非常深厚。五十年代，鄉下解放，沒有田耕，沒有生活費，便和丈夫一起來香港，落地生根，找了一份車衣的工作，幫補家計，為子女供書教學，後來亦做「穿膠花」的工作。當時每個月的人工只有兩三塊，蠻辛苦。下班後能享天倫，已覺得很快樂。現在子女都長大了，有空便到老人中心做義工，或是跟朋友聊天，有時候也會參加一些興趣班，學英文、學電腦。至於孫兒，就很喜歡我弄些小菜給他們吃。我最喜歡就是煮【煎蛋角】給他們吃，拌飯吃最好，有營養又經濟。後來請了菲律賓工人，我就少煮了。每逢新年、八月十五也會慶祝，一家團聚吃飯飲茶。年紀大了，漸漸覺得節日喜慶不太重要。

1967年5月香港爆發工會運動。有說這是受著中國大陸文化大革命的影響，而展開對抗英國殖民政府的暴動。事件最初只是罷工、示威，後期發生暗殺、放置炸彈等事件。51人在暴動中喪生，另超過800人受傷。

甘樹英 七十七歲 祖籍新興

The police were throwing smoke bombs out on the streets. It was horrifying. That was time of the 1967 riots. I can still remember what the explosions sounded like. I grew up on the mainland. My family had a hawker stall selling food. I sometimes helped out. I also worked in the fields, growing vegetables, fertilising the soil and cutting the grass. Children

In May 1967, a trade union-driven social movement took place in Hong Kong, which resulted in anti-British-colonial government riots. The movement began as a series of strikes and demonstrations, and developed into assassinations and bomb attacks.

nowadays have many toys, but we didn't. My friends and I spent our leisure time skipping rope, swallow-shooting and playing on swings. I didn't finish primary school because my family couldn't afford the fees. My parents introduced my future husband to me. He was in the Chinese herbal medicine business, and we grew up in the same village. We developed a strong and deep relationship. We came to Hong Kong in the 1950s, after the countryside was liberated by the communists, because there was no land to farm. After we settled in Hong Kong, I found a job as a seamstress to help pay for our children's education. I also made flowers out of plastic. The monthly income was only about two or three dollars. Life was tough, but we were happy because we could spend time together. My children are all grown up now. When I have time, I volunteer at a home for the elderly. Sometimes, I join groups to learn English and how to use computers. My grandchildren love it when I cook for them. I like making Fried Egg Wrap with Minced Pork. We have family dinners during Chinese New Year and the Mid-Autumn Festival.

Kam Shu Ying 77 year old Hometown Xinxing

煎蛋角

蛋2隻
瘦肉50克
洋蔥1/2個（小）
鹽1/4茶匙
生抽、糖各1/2茶匙
粟粉1茶匙
芫茜數條

1 蛋打勻加鹽1/4茶匙
2 洋蔥去皮，洗淨，切碎
3 瘦肉洗淨、抹乾、切碎，加調味攪勻*
4 洋蔥爆香，加瘦肉同炒熟，備用
5 加油1/2湯匙於鑊內，燒熱後加1湯匙蛋液，煎成小蛋皮
6 加入1茶匙碎肉，把蛋皮覆摺做成小蛋角
7 重複以上做法，至材料用完

* 可用雞蓉代替豬肉，以芫茜上碟裝飾

Fried Egg Wrap with Minced Pork

2 eggs
50 g lean pork*
½ small onion
¼ tsp salt
½ tsp each light soy sauce and sugar
1 tsp cornstarch
some parsley

1 Whisk eggs, add ¼ tsp of salt.
2 Peel onion, wash and chop.
3 Rinse meat, wipe-dry. Chop roughly. Add seasoning and mix well.
4 Stir-fry onion until fragrant. Add chopped meat and fry until cooked. Set aside.
5 Heat wok with ½ tbsp of oil. Add 1 tbsp of egg mixture.
6 As the egg is almost cooked, place 1 tsp of meat filling in centre and fold into a crescent.
7 Repeat until the ingredients are used up. Garnish with parsley.

* *Chicken can be substituted for pork.*

日本軍在船上給難民派發牛奶
和一大條的長麵包。

The Japanese distributed milk and long pieces of bread to all those on board.

賴珍　八十歲　祖籍東莞

父親做生意，我自小便有工人使喚。小時候，整天就跟著大姐、妹妹和弟弟玩耍，到了十歲才進義學讀書。只讀了一個學期，戰爭便開始了。當時跟一位老師在石塘咀上過「卜卜齋」，與老師的兩個女兒一同學習。後來，聽街坊說老師的家被炮彈打中，炮彈從露台穿過另一邊的廚房，老師的兩個女兒都死掉，他就瘋了，自此就與老師失去聯絡。幸好家裡還有點錢，我的一家才不用吃樹皮，但看到無數人為了爭米飯而互相殘殺，多可怕。日軍登陸香港期間，我只有八、九歲，家住西營盤，居住的地方有一個小露台。有一次從露台向下望，見到街上有一個人邊走邊抬著一包大米。突然間，不知哪裡來的一下槍聲「砰」，那個抬米的人便應聲倒地。路旁有一個人衝出來，想要把地上的大米抱走，可是他走了不遠又給子彈打死了。一包大米就要死掉好幾個人。一年後，我與家人乘坐日軍為難民而設的大船返回家鄉。日本軍在船上給難民派發牛奶和一大條的長麵包。在蛇口落船後，我還要走好一大段路才到達家鄉東莞，沿途就看到不少因走難而被遺棄的破房子，牆身都佈滿子彈痕跡。為了省時趕路，我與家人隨身帶備被鋪和乾糧，累了便在街上或破房子中休息，餓了就吃日本軍派的一砵【難民粥】。記得那難民粥是用蜆或蠔肉煮成的。幾經艱苦，我們一家終於回到東莞。父親在鄉間有田有地，生活自然不成問題。在鄉下待了三年多，一家人又回到香港。走難的生活實在太苦了，本來我有兩個妹妹和一個弟弟，走到香港，就只剩下我和弟弟，兩個妹妹都活不下來。我在香港一直沒有工作，閒時除了游水和看戲外，最喜歡就是跟幾位朋友在家中做些縫紉小手作，學會了不少做衫的技巧。廿三歲那年結婚，婚後一直在家中照顧兒女，他們的校服都由我親手縫製而成。如今，兒孫滿堂，家人每次回來吃飯也要預備數十人的分量，就連餸菜也要分三天購買。其中一味【冬菇髮菜蠔豉燜海參】，是我最拿手的菜式，每次用上一斤冬菇都會被吃個精光呢！

糧食短缺時，大米特別珍貴，往往一小杯生米就加水煮成多碗稀粥。更艱苦時有人甚至會於粥水中混入泥沙來填飽肚子。

When I was young, my father had his own business in Hong Kong and we had domestic helpers. I used to play with my older sister, five younger sisters and two younger brothers. I went to school when I was ten, but after only one semester, the war began and so I started studying with a teacher in Shek Tong Tsui who was also teaching her two daughters. One

day, I heard from neighbours that the house had been hit by bombs. One went through the balcony into the kitchen and killed the two girls. The teacher went mad. We were lucky to have some money, so we didn't have to eat tree bark like some poor people. It wasn't uncommon for people to kill each other for rice. It was horrible. One day, I looked down from the balcony where we lived in Sai Ying Pun and saw a man carrying a big bag of rice. Suddenly, there was a gunshot, and he fell down. Another man came running towards the bag of rice and tried to grab it, but there was another gunshot and he fell down dead as well. All for a bag of rice. About a year after the Japanese landed, they offered to ship people back to the mainland, so my family got on one of the boats. They distributed milk and long pieces of bread to all those on board. We got off at Shekou in Guangdong, but there was still a long walk to get to our hometown of Dongguan. We carried blankets and dried food with us. Along the way, we saw many abandoned houses full of bullet holes. When we got tired, we slept on the streets or in old houses. When we were hungry, we ate what's called Refugee Congee that the Japanese distributed. It was made with baby oysters or clams. After much hardship, we reached Dongguan. My father had some farmland there, so life wasn't bad. We stayed there for about three years, then tried to make our way back to Hong Kong. Of all my brothers and sisters, only one of my brothers and I survived the war. I couldn't find work in Hong Kong. A lot of the time I went swimming, and sometimes watched movies. I liked it when my friends and I sewed at home, which is how I learned to make clothes. I got married when I was twenty-three and have looked after my children ever since. I made all their school uniforms. Now, I have grandchildren as well. When the whole family comes home for dinner, I have to prepare food for dozens of people. I have to shop for three whole days to buy everything I need. The dish I make best is Stewed Sea Cucumbers Braised with Winter Mushrooms, Black Moss and Dried Oysters. I use a whole catty (600 grams) of winter mushrooms—and it's devoured in no time!

When food was scarce, rice was especially precious. A small cup of rice could be turned into many bowls of thin congee. In times of poverty, people sometimes mixed the rice with sand and mud.

冬菇髮菜蠔豉燜海參

海參320克（約半斤）
冬菇6-8隻
髮菜少許
蠔豉160克（約4兩）
薑2片
蔥2條
蒜頭160克（約4兩）
果皮1片（浸軟去囊）
調味：適量糖、鹽、蠔油、柱侯醬、大地魚粉及胡椒粉

1 海參*用猛火燒到通紅，用水浸兩日，每天換水一次
2 把海參放進沸水中，蓋上蓋，焗至水變冷為止
3 用水清洗，重複焗水的步驟，直至海參變軟
4 把海參剖開，去內臟，用薑蔥水汆水，瀝乾水分備用
5 髮菜用水浸軟，加油數滴，用手搓髮菜除污，過清水備用
6 冬菇浸軟去蒂備用
7 蠔豉略浸擦，洗淨
8 放少許油於鍋中，爆香薑、蔥、蒜頭、柱侯醬，加入大地魚粉、胡椒粉、果皮、水及蠔豉一齊煲
9 下海參、冬菇一同燜至入味
10 放進糖、鹽、蠔油、髮菜一起燜至汁濃，便可食用

* 海參可選用石柱參或豬婆參
鳴謝：陳錦成師傅（翠亨村大廚）提供烹調方法

Stewed Sea Cucumber Braised with Winter Mushrooms, Black Moss and Dried Oysters

320 g sea cucumbers
6-8 winter mushrooms
some black moss
160 g dried oysters
2 slices ginger
2 spring onions
160 g garlic
1 aged tangerine peel
(soak and scrape off the inner membrane)
seasoning : some sugar, salt, oyster sauce, braised beef paste, *dae di* (flounder) fish powder, pepper

1 Pan-fry sea cucumbers on high heat until red. Soak in water for two days, changing water once a day.
2 Put sea cucumbers into water and bring to a boil. Keep cover on until it becomes cold, then rinse with water.
3 Repeat until sea cucumbers become soft.
4 Cut sea cucumbers length-wise, discard the membrane and intestines. Blanch with half the ginger and spring onions. Drain and set aside.
5 Soak black moss until soft. Add a few drops of oil, squeeze by hand to clean, then rinse.
6 Soak mushrooms until soft and discard the stems.
7 Soak dried oysters for a while. Rub and rinse.
8 Stir-fry the remaining ginger, spring onions, garlic and braised beef paste in wok with a little oil. Add *dae di* fish powder, pepper, aged tangerine peel, dried oysters and water. Bring to a boil.
9 Add sea cucumbers and mushrooms. Simmer until soft.
10 Add sugar, salt, oyster sauce and black moss. Simmer until sauce thickens. Serve.

Thanks to Mr. Chan Kam Shing, Head of Chef of Tsui Hang Village Restaurant for the recipe.

難民粥（蠔仔粥）

大地魚肉或魚乾50克
冬菇3粒
中國芹菜3段
肉碎50克
蠔仔150克*
飯1碗
冬菜、蒜蓉、雞精少許
上湯1/2杯
魚露2茶匙

1 先將肉碎、蠔仔*汆水備用
2 用少許油將蒜蓉爆香
3 加入上湯**、飯、冬菇、冬菜、芹菜及大地魚
4 用魚露、雞精調味，加入蠔仔
5 湯滾後即可享用

* 用疏窿筲箕盛住蠔仔浸於水中輕搖，可搖去沙石而不會把蠔仔弄破。沖水時要不停搖動筲箕，方能除去污物
** 一鍋靚的蠔仔粥，湯底至為重要。師傅採用大地魚、豬骨、雞、大豆芽及胡椒粒煲4小時成為湯底，再加入白飯、蠔仔、冬菇絲、肉碎、蝦米、冬菜、蔥等材料

Refugee (Baby Oyster) Congee

some *dae di* fish
3 winter mushrooms
3 stalks Chinese celery
50 g minced pork
150 g baby oysters*
1 bowl cooked rice
some spiced cabbage, chicken powder and minced garlic
½ cup chicken broth**
2 tsp fish sauce

1 Blanch baby oysters and minced pork in water. Drain and set aside.
2 In a heated wok, stir-fry minced garlic with a little oil until fragrant.
3 Add chicken broth, rice, mushrooms, spiced cabbage, Chinese celery and *dae di*.
4 Add rice and water. Stir.
5 Add fish sauce and chicken powder to taste.
6 Finally, add baby oysters and minced pork. Serve after boiling.

** Rinse baby oysters in a medium-hole strainer, gently shaking to sift away sand and stone without cracking them.*
*** For best results, make your own soup base. Cook dae di fish, pork bone, chicken, soya bean sprouts and peppercorn in water for four hours. Then add rice, baby oysters, shredded mushrooms, minced pork, dried shrimp, spiced cabbage and chopped spring onion, etc.*

那時候有日本軍人帶著劍槍來理髮，
嚇得理髮師傅手忙腳亂……

I still remember the Japanese with their rifles
coming for a haircut.

何淑芳 八十三歲 祖籍中山

小時候家裡是開理髮店的。我是家中獨女，既不用做家務，也不用到店子裡幫忙。因為父親早去世，店子就由母親和祖母負責打理，理髮師傅都是請回來打工的。那是一間小型理髮店，店前面是做理髮的，有三張理髮椅，後面是住家，也就是吃飯睡覺的地方。後來長大了，我便跟親戚去學車衣，二十一歲結婚以後便來了香港定居。雖然曾進學校讀書，但遇上戰爭要走難，最後只讀到小學四年級。當時沒有電視機和收音機，但我對局勢都很清楚。日本軍要來時，學校停課了，我只好無奈地終日留在家中，無所事事。每天我都會聽到飛機在上空隆隆地飛過。還記得，那時候有日本軍人帶著劍槍來理髮，嚇得理髮師傅手忙腳亂，我更怕得躲在床下不敢動。戰爭期間，饑荒和搶掠很平常。小學的時候，我曾在街上買了一條油炸鬼，轉眼就被搶了；所以人們買了東西以後，都緊張地收藏好，尤其是食物。當時的糧食貴得很，十塊錢就只得四兩米。祖母幾經辛苦買到白米，回家後趕忙用禾稈草蓋好，免得被人發現呢。慶幸我們未至於要捱餓。那時，祖母為一家人張羅食物，用有限的材料弄些飽肚的飯菜。印象最深刻的，是【魚腸茄子拌飯】。現代人都怕膽固醇高對身體不好，魚腸之類的內臟都不敢吃太多，我現在都會改用鯪魚肉。用蒜頭和薑蔥把鑊爆香來煮魚腸，魚腸吃起來就不會有腥味。魚腸茄子一起煮得爛熟，夠油膩，拌飯吃一碗比單吃兩碗白飯更飽肚，深受理髮店的伙計歡迎。那是祖母自己想出來的，由祖母親手做的就最好吃！

隨移民潮來港的上海人有的是商人，亦不乏技術人材，理髮師就是其中之一。五六十年代香港上海理髮店盛極一時，帶來新的感覺。那些上海師傅手工精巧，價錢相宜，花得起錢的顧客都會選擇洗剪吹、剃鬚或修甲，甚至清潔耳朵等全套服務，高級的理髮店還會提供按摩服務。當然不會有現代的什麼染髮、洗燙、負離子直髮、陶瓷電髮等服務。

Many Shanghaiese came to Hong Kong in the 1950s and 1960s. Shanghainese barber shops were very popular. They offered hair-dressing, grooming and manicure services.

My family had a barber shop in Shanghai. Even though I was the only daughter, I didn't have to help with chores at home or at the shop. When my father died, my mother and grandmother took care of the shop, which was at the front of our home and had three chairs for hairdressing. We lived at the back. That's where we slept and ate. When I was older,

a relative taught me to sew. I got married when I was twenty-one and came to Hong Kong. Because of the war, I only went to school until Primary Four. The school was closed down when the Japanese came. There was nothing to do but stay at home most of the time. Every day, I heard planes flying overhead. I still remember the Japanese with their rifles coming for a haircut. The hairdressers were so scared. I used to hide under the bed. During the war, famine and robberies were part of daily life. I remember buying fried dough once and someone stealing it from me straight away. When people bought things, they would hide them well, particularly food, which was extremely expensive at that time. Whenever my grandmother bought rice, she would hide it under straw. We were lucky we didn't have empty stomachs. Grandmother was always the one who went about getting food for the family. She used whatever she could find to make food that filled us up. The most memorable dish she made was fish intestines and eggplant with rice. These days, people worry about cholesterol and avoid things like intestines. But they taste good when fried with eggplant, ginger and spring onions. There's no fishy smell. They become greasy when cooked with eggplant. Mixing it with a bowl of rice fills you up more than having two bowls of plain rice. It was very popular with the hairdressers. My grandmother's way of making it is still the best.

Ho Suk Fong 83 years old Hometown Zhongshan

魚鬆茄子拌飯

茄子半個
鯪魚肉150克
米50克
油、胡椒、鹽、蔥花、麻油及豉油少許

1 鯪魚肉剁成蓉，加入調味拌勻，煎好後切成薄長條，備用
2 茄子切成小方塊，混合油、鹽、蔥花，隔水蒸8分鐘，備用
3 飯煮至差不多熟時，加入茄子和鯪魚條，低溫焗5分鐘
4 吃時拌以麻油、蔥花、豉油

Minced Dace and Eggplant with Rice

½ eggplant
150 g dace fillet
50 g long-grain white rice
oil, pepper, salt, spring onions, sesame oil and soy sauce

1. Mince dace fillet. Add pinches of salt, pepper and half of the chopped spring onions. Mix well. Fry until cooked and cut into long, thin slices. Set aside.
2. Cut eggplant into small cubes. Mix with a dab of sesame oil and soy sauce. Steam for eight minutes. Set aside.
3. Cook rice. When water has almost evaporated, put in eggplant and fish slices. Leave on low heat for five minutes.
4. Serve with sesame oil, chopped spring onions and soy sauce.

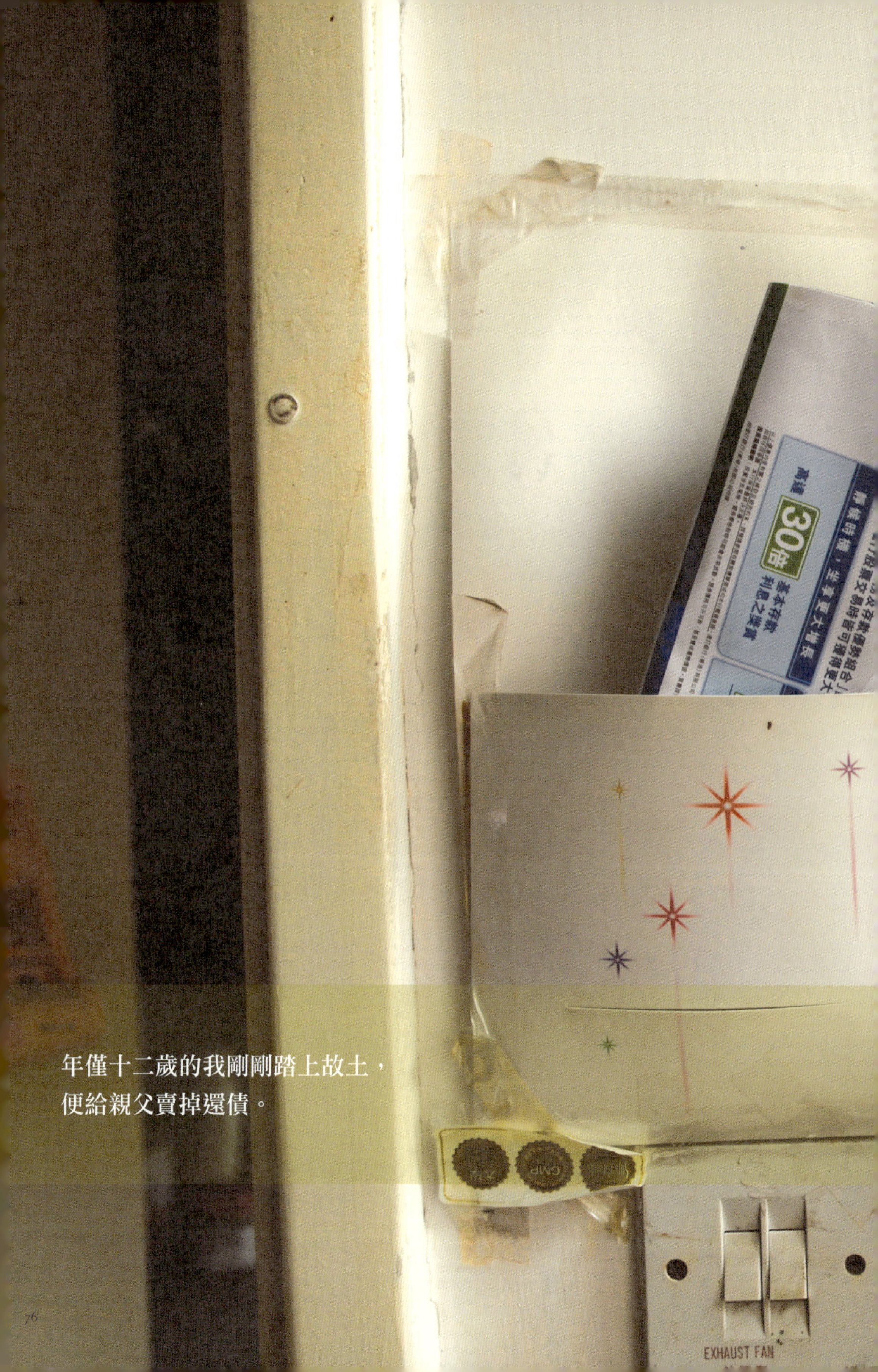

年僅十二歲的我剛剛踏上故土，
便給親父賣掉還債。

He was so deeply in debt from gambling that as soon as I arrived, he sold me. I was twelve.

我才八歲，日本軍攻入廣州，為了逃避戰火，婆婆和姨媽帶同我南來香港。數年後，爸爸說希望我們回鄉一家團聚。誰知這是好賭的他債台高築走投無路的下策，結果年僅十二歲的我剛剛踏上故土，便給親父賣掉還債。七年來不識字的我與媽媽斷絕了音訊，被賣至東莞一戶莫姓人家幫忙幹粗活。耕田看牛的苦日子裡，連一件像樣的衣服也沒有，只有用裝米的「胡椒包」開個洞當作衣服穿；沒有鞋子，赤腳踏著豬糞牛糞，不時弄至爛腳；而經常擔近一百斤番薯藤去餵豬，令我患上肩周炎，現在仍隱隱作痛。記得約在我十六歲那年，東莞發生水災，不少禾田被浸，我們要捱番薯度日。難得有飯吃就一粒米都不會浪費，剩下的飯焦，我們便用蒸熟了的番薯混成【番薯粥】吃。我寧願吃番薯，混著濕濕的較容易吞。養母二娘會將炒米餅收藏在閣子，只在特別時節才拿出來。一天我趁二娘不在家就偷偷取了一片，也不敢立刻「毀屍滅跡」，便藏在褲頭中，沒料到竟然遲不該早不該就在二娘面前掉了下來，不用說自然招來一頓毒打。好專制的，二娘吃時別人才可以吃。姨媽一直很關顧我們一家，知道我媽媽和哥哥在廣州幫人倒夜香和搬大石為生，便申請他們到香港，剛剛在共產黨來之前離開。他們當時在灣仔落腳，輾轉竟碰上我的養父二叔，媽媽便急不及待問他。她說：「莫先生，我的阿妹怎樣了？讓我見見她吧！」養父就以三百港元讓我贖身。我到達香港一見媽媽，便哭如淚人。我一句廣東話也不懂，滿口東莞鄉下話。幸好疼惜我的堂家姐耐心地跟我練習，又指吃【豆腐花】可以幫助我快點學懂廣東話，經常讓我一飽口福。到現在我仍然相信豆腐花有神奇功效呢。我自二十歲起便打住家工，遇上當船公司經理的「好事頭」，想我識字，供我唸夜學。我一向不喜歡唸書，上了幾堂，因害怕老師叫我寫黑板便逃學，現在不識字囉。廿一歲那年經媒人介紹，下嫁了給一名補鞋匠，不過我們經已分開近四十年。這段「捱了許多鹹苦」的婚姻給了我兩子一女。我的拿手小菜其實當時孩子都沒機會吃，生活清苦時，「一蚊雞」就是一家一天的餸錢，只夠買兩隻鹹蛋、三毛叉燒、幾條白菜之類果腹。我一大清早出門工作至五時多，然後到街市買餸，回家飲杯水休息一下，便開始弄飯。現在我閒來會幫忙街坊帶小孩。孩子都讚我：婆婆弄的雞翼很好吃！我都只隨便弄弄吧。我會到街市凍肉鋪買大約十隻雞翼，將雞翼洗淨晾乾後，用拍扁了的蒜頭和薑，加油爆香雞翼，倒進一個煲內，再加入適量的老抽和糖，及少許水焗一會，一道好味又簡單的焗雞翼便大功告成了。另外一款我拿手的是紅衫魚湯。我會把煲薯仔的水加到剛煎好的魚中，湯便會變成如牛奶一般的奶白色，然後放進薯仔煲中。這些「餐頭湯」不用煮太久，一個鐘頭便很好味，頂呱呱！

原為「一文雞」，粵語會把「文」讀為「蚊」。「文」是古代銀兩的一種單位。有說上世紀初在香港的塘西召妓，有規定格式的「花紙」，需先寫自已名號，然後寫上妓女名字，寫好以後交由酒樓雜役帶去妓院，那些阿姑接到「花紙」，便應召「出局」。每次局票收取一元，而廣府人稱妓女為「雞」。今天說的「一蚊雞」，只是港幣一元的意思。

李妹女　八十歲　祖籍新會

My father was a dreadful gambler. We had to rely on what my mother and brother made selling vegetables. When I was eight, the Japanese made their way into Guangzhou. My grandmother brought the three of us to Hong Kong, leaving father behind. A few years later, my father invited us back home for a reunion. It turned out to be a trick. He was so deeply in debt from gambling that as soon as I arrived, he sold me. I was twelve. For seven years, I lost contact with my mother and brother because I didn't know how to write. I was sold to a family in Dongguan to work in the fields. During all those bitter days, they never even gave me decent clothes to wear. I used to cut holes and wear rice bags to cover myself. I had no shoes to wear, so my feet often hurt from treading in the excrement of pigs and cows. My shoulder also became infected from carrying sweet potatoes to the animals. It still hurts to this day. When I was sixteen, there was a bad flood in Dongguan. Many fields were inundated. Most of the time, we only had sweet potatoes. When there was rice, we made sure we didn't waste a single grain. We would add steamed sweet potatoes to the burnt rice at the bottom of the pot and put in water to make sweet potato congee. The woman who raised me would hide fried rice cakes in the attic and take them out only on special occasions. One day I stole a piece when she wasn't at home and hid it in my pants. But when she came back, it dropped out right in front of her! I got a painful beating. My aunt cared about our family a lot. She helped us apply to come to Hong Kong. That was just before the Communists came to power. We lived in Wanchai. My own mother had been asking about my whereabouts. Eventually, she paid the family $300 to set me free—ten times what my father had sold me for. When my mother and I were reunited in Hong Kong, we couldn't stop crying. Back then, I didn't know even one Cantonese phrase. Even now, I still have a heavy Dongguan accent. My cousin used to patiently coach me in Cantonese. She used to feed me sweet soup with bean curd because she said that eating it would help me learn Cantonese. I still believe in its magic power. I worked as a domestic helper from the time I was about twenty. I had a good boss, who was the manager of a shipping company. He wanted me to learn writing and encouraged me to study at evening school. But I've never liked studying. After a few classes, I was afraid the teacher would ask me to write on the blackboard, so I ran away. When I was twenty-one, I was introduced to a shoe-maker. We got married but we have been separated for more than forty years. The marriage caused me lots of bitterness, but it also gave me two sons and a daughter. We were very poor, and we had only one dollar each day to spend on food. That would buy two salty eggs, a few cents worth of roast pork and a few *pak choi* leaves. I usually went to work early in the morning and finished at about five in the afternoon. I would get groceries from the market on the way home. After sitting down to have a glass of water, I'd start cooking. Nowadays, I often help my neighbours take care of their children. They would say, "Grandma makes delicious chicken wings!" They are not so difficult to make. I usually buy about ten chicken wings at the market. You rinse them well and dry them, then heat a pot and put in garlic and ginger. Then you add oil and put in the chicken wings. Next, you add dark soy sauce, sugar and a bit of water, and let it stew for a while. It's a simple, tasty dish. Another dish I'm good at is soup with red mullet. I save the water from boiling potatoes and put it into a pot with fish that has been fried well. The soup becomes as white as milk. Perfect!

香滑豆腐花

原味豆漿600毫升(500毫升+100毫升)
熟石膏粉1/4茶匙
鷹粟粉11/2茶匙
水200毫升
薑及片糖各1-2片

1 熟石膏粉*及鷹粟粉拌勻，再加100毫升豆漿拌勻成粉漿待用
2 豆漿500毫升煲熱後立即熄火
3 熱豆漿和粉漿同時從高處倒入器皿內(約1呎以上，左右手並用)，立刻蓋上蓋子，不動，等20分鐘
4 水、薑、片糖，煲成糖水，吃時加入豆腐花內**

* 熟石膏粉可在中藥店買到，買10元用盒子盛起可供多次使用
** 可鹹吃，上面放麻油、蔥花、頭抽及小撮碎鹹菜，是最適合夏天吃的醒胃小吃

Fragrant and Silky Bean Curd Dessert

600 ml plain soya milk
¼ tsp food grade gypsum powder
1½ tsps cornstarch
200 ml water
1-2 pieces each sliced ginger and slab of sugar

1 Mix and stir food grade gypsum powder* and cornstarch. Add in 100 ml soya milk. Mix and stir into paste. Set aside.
2 Heat 500 ml soya milk. When boiled, turn off heat.
3 From a height of at least 1 foot, and, using both hands, pour hot soya milk and paste into a deep container. Cover with lid at once; let it stand for 20 mins.
4 Boil water with ginger and slab sugar to make sweet soup. Add into mixture of soya milk and paste.** Serve.

* *Food grade gypsum powder can be purchased at Chinese herbal stores.*
** *Silky bean curd can be served with salt—spread mixture with some sesame oil, chopped spring onion, premium soy sauce and a pinch of chopped spiced vegetables. This could be a good appetizer in the summer.*

番薯粥

米1/3杯
番薯2隻
紅棗數粒
薑2片
水10杯
鹽1/4茶匙
油少許

1 將米洗淨，加少量鹽、油及水浸3小時
2 放入適量水於鍋內，下薑片及米煮至滾起，轉慢火煮約1小時
3 番薯去皮洗淨切成小塊，用清水浸半小時；紅棗洗淨
4 將上述材料加入粥中，用中小火煲至粥米開花，番薯腍軟即可*
5 粥煮成後，無須下鹽，可清吃或配任何餸菜吃

* 下番薯後要小心火的控制，以免黏著鍋底

Sweet Potato Congee

⅓ cup rice
2 sweet potatoes
few red dates
2 slices ginger
10 cups of water
salt and oil

1 Rinse rice. Add a few pinches of salt, a tablespoon of oil and some water at the top of the rice and soak for three hours.
2 Pour into a pot 10 cups of water to make congee. Add rice and ginger. Bring the water to a rolling boil, then reset to low heat and cook for about an hour*.
3 Peel sweet potatoes and cut into small pieces. Soak in water for half an hour. Rinse red dates.
4 Add sweet potatoes and dates to the pot of congee. Cook on low-to-medium heat until the sweet potatoes are soft and the congee rice cracks.
5 Serve as it is or with other dishes.

* *Watch the heat carefully to prevent the congee from sticking to the bottom of the pot.*

不記得多少次要帶著弟妹躲到山上……

Often I hid my young brother and three sisters
in the hills to protect them and
brought them home only when it was dark.

我只懂煮西餐，中餐太難的菜式我是不懂得弄的。小時，我家在新會鄉下都算有點錢，有兩個妹仔（女傭人），爸爸當老師，媽媽在家料理家務，有空便打牌消閒。我三歲便開始上學，可惜好景不常，十二歲那年中國解放，爸爸在外國打工。我家本為地主，解放時成為批鬥目標。所有值錢的東西也被人拿走，連爸爸寄回來的錢都被搶去。平日亦不好受，常常被貧農欺負，例如擲石頭。不記得多少次要帶著弟妹躲到山上，待天黑才敢回家。最意外的，是大妹仔反過來鬥我媽媽。當時妹仔出嫁，媽媽送禮金不少，想不到她會這樣做，差點把媽媽氣死！媽媽受盡折磨，想過自殺，但想到自己還有兒女需要撫養，才打消這個念頭，繼續獨自養大我們。我有三妹一弟，年紀輕輕就要去賣柴。一早四點多便要起床上山斬柴，雙手都花了。無辦法，沒錢，做大的，一定要做。幸好當時我們有田地，每餐可以吃自己種的東西，常吃的是【南瓜拌飯】。每天如事，直至我十三歲，廣州優待華僑，成立了「華僑局」，我們一家就申請到廣州。小妹仔聽從她的朋友規勸，與其留下沒東西吃，不如一走了之，不久，她便悄悄離開了。媽媽和弟妹一個一個先後逃到廣州。我熱愛讀書，完成了中三才去。到達廣州，起初日子也難熬。一張糧票只能換三十斤米，可要維持全家人一年的食用。那麼多弟妹，哪裡夠吃呢！幸好那時候爸爸能夠順利寄錢回來，才能買黑市米吃，不用捱餓。往後日子漸露曙光。我在廣州依然不忘讀書，一有機會便想上學。中學時，我認識現在的丈夫，之後因拍拖沒心機讀書，十六歲便跟著他來港，二十一歲便結婚了。到港後，我又再掀起讀書的念頭。在民生英文書院讀過兩年書。八六年，我還到美國住了七年，入了籍。但是始終覺得不適合，便決定回港定居。我的孫兒卻比較喜歡美國，每次回來香港，都嚷著要回去。我很高興現在有兩兒兩女，六個孫兒，加上我和丈夫二人，剛好湊夠一打！

解放前，很多中國人簽了合同，到南洋或美國等地從事如採礦等苦工，俗稱「賣豬仔」。有人客死異鄉，也有人衣錦還鄉。

The good times didn't last. China was liberated when I was twelve. At the time, my father was working overseas. Because my family belonged to the land-owning class, we became targets for criticism. All our valuables were taken away, including the money my father sent us. We were bullied and had stones thrown at us by the peasants. Often I hid my

Before 1949, many Chinese signed contracts to work as manual workers (such as at mines) in the US and other places. This is colloquially known as "selling the pigs abroad". Some workers died overseas. Others returned with a fortune.

young brother and three sisters in the hills to protect them and brought them home only when it was dark. Even our eldest *mui tsai* [household servant] turned against us. My mother almost died of rage! She thought about killing herself, but she carried on bringing us up on her own. I used to sell firewood. I would get up at four in the morning and climb the mountains to get the wood. I also caught little crabs to sell. I had scratches all over my hands, but I was the eldest, and I had to do something for the family. We could still have Rice and Pumpkin most days. It's now one of my favourite dishes. When I was thirteen, my family applied to go to Guangzhou. Life there wasn't easy in the beginning. One food ration ticket was good for only 30 catties of rice—and that was for the whole family for one year! Luckily, my father was able to get money to us. We were able to buy rice from the black market to keep our stomachs full, and our lives began to improve. I met my future husband there when I was in secondary school. I became distracted when we started courting. When I was sixteen, I came to Hong Kong with him. We got married when I turned twenty-one. In 1986, I went to the US, stayed there for seven years and obtained citizenship. But I didn't feel right, so I returned to Hong Kong. I'm so glad I have two sons, two daughters and six grandchildren. Together with my husband, that makes one whole dozen of us in the family!

鹽焗雞

光雞1隻*
薑2片
蔥2條
焗雞用的粗鹽適量
沙紙數張
鹽適量

1 光雞斬去腳爪，抹乾，用鹽擦遍雞身內外
2 將薑、蔥放入雞肚內，用數張沙紙包裹著雞
3 將粗鹽放入鑊內，炒至熱騰騰
4 用鑊鏟在鹽中間挖一大洞，把雞（雞胸朝下）埋入鹽中
5 上面再用鹽覆蓋著，焗至雞全熟**
6 將雞取出，趁熱斬件上碟，配沙薑油蘸吃

* 如雞重900克（約2磅），焗的時間約需30分鐘
** 如粗鹽不夠熱，可取出雞，炒熱鹽，再焗

鳴謝：翁仰光先生（富豪酒家/阿翁鮑魚行政總裁）提供烹調方法

Chicken Baked in Rock Salt

1 whole chicken*
2 pieces of ginger
2 stalks spring onion
some rock salt, specially for baking chicken
several sheets of steaming paper
some salt

1 Rinse chicken, remove nails, and wipe dry. Rub chicken (inside and out) with salt.
2 Stuff ginger and spring onion into chicken cavity. Wrap the whole chicken with several sheets of slightly greased steaming paper.
3 Put a substantial amount of rock salt into wok and fry until they get steaming hot.
4 Make a hole in the centre of the salt heap and bury chicken (breast down) in the salt. Cover the top with more hot rock salt** and bake until cooked.
5 Take out chicken, unwrap and cut into pieces. To serve, dip with finely chopped ginger and spring onion in hot oil.

** For a whole chicken of 900 g (2 lbs), baking time takes around 30 mins.*
*** If rock salt gets cold, take out chicken and repeat Steps 3 & 4.*

Thanks to Mr. Yung, Managing Direction of Fu Ho Restaurant for the recipe.

南瓜拌飯

南瓜1片
米50克
白菜葉1片
鹽、油、上湯適量

1 南瓜去皮後，取一小片切成碎粒
2 白米洗淨，加湯泡後，放在電飯煲內煮*
3 待水沸後加入南瓜粒、白菜葉煮至米、瓜糜爛
4 略加油、鹽調味即可食用

* 可混和紅米一同煮吃，更健康和有營養

Rice and Pumpkin

1 slice pumpkin
50 g long-grain rice*
1 slice long cabbage, finely chopped
some salt, oil and clear broth

1 Peel pumpkin. Take one slice and dice.
2 Rinse rice, add clear broth and put in rice cooker.
3 After water boils, add diced pumpkin and long cabbage. Cook until cabbage and pumpkin are soft.
4 Add a few dashes of oil and salt to taste.

** It's more nutritious to mix red rice with white rice.*

那些日子兵荒馬亂，聽著磨芝麻的聲音，
竟令人平靜下來。

Those were difficult times, but as I quietly stirred the soup, listening to the scratching of the sesame against the pot, I felt calm.

我今年八十二歲，有四個孩子六個孫了。哈哈！都是靠倒垃圾養大他們的。那時一日做五份工，哪裡管得孩子的吃喝。更慘的人都有，鄰家一整家人吃了竹樹花，就肚子撐脹死掉。打仗時，我們一家十一個兄弟姊妹齊齊從鄉下來香港。父親早就不在，母親的負擔可想而知。「三年零八個月」粥水也無得吃。怎辦？十多口擠在大角咀一間唐樓，餓了幾日，嫂嫂有了BB更慘，幸好母親從荃灣擔了些自己種植的花生與芝麻出來賣。一家人吃過花生醬，也吃過荳醬，那是磨了油剩下來的渣滓！我家日日都是食這兩味，有時會做【芝麻糊】或花生糊。我小時候已很頑皮，人家騎牛，我女仔人家就企在牛背上。如何發泄過盛的精力呢？家人就叫我這個野孩子幫手擂芝麻糊。幾十年前要吃芝麻糊殊不容易，非要用上「擂漿棍」，在有粗紋的沙盤上擂呀擂，攪上半天才磨出一頓美味的芝麻糊呢！儘管那些日子兵荒馬亂，默默攪動擂漿棍，聽著磨芝麻的聲音，竟令人平靜下來。若把黑芝麻先炒香，口感更佳，煮時加入片糖和薑慢慢攪拌。不要看它黑麻麻的，勝在心地挺好，點滴散發著對孩子的關愛。

1941年12月25日至1945年8月15日，日本佔領香港。期間，日軍在港殺人無數，民不聊生。直至美軍以原子彈轟炸長崎，日本宣布投降，第二次世界大戰結束，英國才重掌香港的主權。

黃翠萍　八十二歲　祖籍三水

I have four children and six grandchildren. When the children were young, we lived on scraps. I collected garbage and worked at five jobs a day to make ends meet. How could I have time to think about what they ate? But I knew people who fared even worse. I saw my neighbours eat flowers from bamboo trees. Their bellies swelled up and they died.

During the war, our entire family of eleven came to Hong Kong from Sansui, our hometown. My father died when I was young. You can imagine what a burden this put on my mother. There was often nothing to eat—not even thin porridge. We were stuck in an apartment in Tai Kok Tsui. We often had empty stomachs. It was even worse when my sister-in-law got pregnant. Mother sometimes brought home peanuts and sesame she had planted to sell. We would eat peanut butter and bean paste, which is the residue left from extracting oil from peanuts. Since peanuts and sesame were all we had, we made them into sweet sesame and peanut soups. I was very naughty as a girl. I had so much energy and was always looking for ways to let it out. People would call me a wild child. To quiet me down, sometimes I was told to help grind the sesame soup. I stirred and stirred the sesame in a rough sandy pot. It took half a day to make it into a smooth, tasty soup! It took a lot of effort to make this delicacy. Those were difficult times, but as I quietly stirred the soup, listening to the scratching of the sesame against the pot, I felt calm. That was the only time I made sweet sesame soup in all these years. But childhood memories last forever. Frying black sesame with half a portion of rice flour gives the soup more texture. Use only cane sugar, and slowly stir in ginger. Don't judge it by its dark appearance—it has a very kind heart!

Wong Chui Ping 82 years old Hometown Sansui

芝麻糊

黑芝麻320克（約半斤）
粘米160克（約4兩）
片糖4片
水1公升
薑1片

1 粘米洗淨，浸4－5小時，瀝乾水分
2 白鑊炒香黑芝麻，洗淨備用
3 把粘米、黑芝麻、水放入攪拌機內磨成漿，隔渣
4 將芝麻漿加片糖、薑，煮滾至糖溶便成*

* 煮時慢慢攪拌，可令芝麻糊更滑

Sesame Sweet Soup

320 g black sesame
160 g white long-grain rice
4 slabs of sugar
1 litre water
1 piece ginger

1 Wash and soak the rice for four to five hours, then drain.
2 Roast black sesame in a dry wok. Rinse and set aside.
3 Put water, black sesame and rice into blender. Blend until smooth, then strain.
4 Add the sugar and ginger to the sesame paste. Bring to a boil*. When sugar is melted, it's ready to serve.

** Stir slowly while boiling gives a smoother paste.*

都是捱回來的，算是很好的了。

Much of my early life was spent alone and miserable.
Now, I have a family of ten.
For me, it's quite a blessing.

日本仔要入城喇！我由江門走難到新會，經澳門到香港，再輾轉返回澳門。我小時候，母親意外懷了新孕產下弟弟，她半年後卻因體弱而過身。因為家貧，家人把弟弟送走。爸爸更突然失蹤，大概是在戰爭中死去吧。就這樣，家裡霎時間只剩我一人。家散人亡，我被帶到嬸嬸家，便跟嬸嬸做一些手作，也在工廠做了一段時間雜工。當時很窮很窮，一個月也沒有一餐米吃，天天捱飢抵餓。那時候，辛辛苦苦掙回來的食物會被人強搶去，很是悽涼。後來，我打算到海南島去，船也上了，因中途船上缺糧，只好泊岸，我下船買食物，碰上一名朋友，他勸我不要到海南島去，因為那裡的人說的話我聽不懂，沒法生存，還說會介紹工作給我。於是，我孑然一身，行李也沒有從船上拿回來，便留在廣州跟那個朋友一起住了。過了九年，有位在香港的姊妹邀請我去探訪她，結果從此在港定居。我經朋友介紹認識了丈夫，誕下三個兒子。現在丈夫過了身，閒時我喜歡入廚煮些小菜給孫兒吃。四歲的小孫女最愛吃我弄的菜，尤其喜歡吃鴨舌。孫仔卻喜歡吃雞翼，我便把兩樣混起來煮，自創一道菜【滷水鴨舌雞翼】。由孑然一身，到現在一家十一口，都是捱回來的，算是很好的了。

第二次世界大戰後，國共內戰，大量民眾湧入香港避難。移民潮為香港帶來廉價的勞動力、技術和資金，成為香港發展的重要基石。

My mother died six months after giving birth to my brother. My family was so poor that he was soon sent away to be adopted. Then my father went missing. He probably died in the war. So, I was the only one left. I was sent to live with my aunt in Xinhui. At first, I worked with her making handicrafts at home, and then at a factory. We were very poor. We

couldn't even afford one meal of rice a month. I often had an empty stomach. Sometimes, people robbed me of food I'd worked hard for. It was so miserable. I decided to go to Hainan and managed to get onboard a ship, but there was nothing to eat. When the ship stopped in Guangzhou, I got off to get food. By chance, I ran into a friend. He told me not to go to Hainan because I didn't know the language and wouldn't survive. He said he would find work for me. I didn't even bother going back to the ship for my meagre belongings. Nine years later, a girlfriend in Hong Kong invited me to visit her, and I simply stayed on. Eventually, a friend introduced me to my future husband. We got married and I eventually gave birth to three sons. My husband is dead now, but I still cook for my grandchildren. My four-year-old granddaughter loves my cooking, especially Stewed Duck Tongues and Chicken Wings in Chinese Marinade. Much of my early life was spent alone and miserable. Now, I have a family of ten. For me, it's quite a blessing.

After the Second World War, many people left China to come to Hong Kong. They became a labour force vital to the development of Hong Kong.

滷水鴨舌雞翼

雞翼10隻
鴨舌250克
滷水汁半支（200毫升）
滷水料：黃糖1湯匙，水8杯，
生抽1杯半，老抽1/2杯
香料：草果2粒，甘草8-9片，八角
9-10粒，桂皮2片，沙薑1/3兩，陳皮
1/3個，紅米2湯匙，玫瑰露酒1/4杯

1 先將雞翼和鴨舌汆水，備用
2 將滷水汁*，連同雞翼和鴨舌一起放進鍋裡
3 滷水汁煲滾後，熄火
4 鍋蓋緊蓋，讓雞翼和鴨舌浸於汁內約20分鐘
5 以慢火煲滾滷水汁，再煮10分鐘

* 如不想使用市面上已製成之滷水汁，可按以上提供之滷水料及香料自製

Stewed Duck Tongues and Chicken Wings in Chinese Marinade

10 chicken wings
250 g duck tongues
200 ml Chinese marinade*

1 Rinse and blanch duck tongues and chicken wings. Rinse well and set aside.
2 Add Chinese marinade to duck tongues and chicken wings in casserole dish.
3 Bring to a boil. Turn off heat.
4 Let duck tongues and chicken wings soak in sauce for 20 minutes, tightly covered.
5 Simmer sauce on low heat for 10 minutes.

** Make your own Chinese marinade with ½ cup dark soy sauce, 1½ cup light soy sauce, 8 cups water and 1 tbsp brown sugar.*

時兒

遊戲

PLaY

我們年紀小，最喜歡和朋友晚上
守在椰樹旁，等椰子蟹來吃椰子。

When I was still young and living in Malaysia,
we used to wait by the coconut trees
for the crabs to come down and eat the coconuts.

容梅仙　終年七十一歲　祖籍中山

從父親口中，得知我才出生，便遇上中日戰爭。走難時實在太窮困，父母親曾痛心地把我遺留在路旁的樹下。他們走了半天的路，委實不忍，終於回頭找我，幸得善心人幫忙，把我尋回，在路旁以溪水為我洗澡，用舊衣服把我包裹起來，一家人又繼續上路，逃難到南洋，十多年後輾轉來到香港。在南洋時，我年紀小，最喜歡和朋友晚上守在椰樹旁，等椰子蟹來吃椰子。牠們的鉗很厲害，「卜」的一聲，椰子就被牠們破開了。等到椰子蟹爬下樹來，我們就把牠們網著，拿回家給媽媽煮。嘩！又有椰香，又有蟹味。香港沒有這種蟹，所以不可能吃到了。我只好把菜式改動一下，來點馬來亞風味，變成了【咖哩蟹】。在香港婚後的日子，幸得夫家愛寵，大家都喜歡我弄的馬來亞風味菜。一天在活動中心說起馬拉盞，有的長者以為是新式茶樓的時尚品種，什麼小馬拉糕呢。不！那其實是一種馬來西亞的調味料。說起甜品的做法，當然除了首選的芝麻糊、杏仁糊之外，還有我拿手的【麼麼咋咋】！有豆，有芋頭，又有牛奶和椰奶。有益又好味。

馬拉盞（Belachan）有說其名字是來自葡萄牙語。製法與蝦醬和蝦膏相似，以小銀蝦和鹽經發酵和生曬製作而成，主要用作配料，可拌飯或炒菜，如馬拉盞炒通菜。

Soon after I was born, the Japanese came and my family fled. Along the way, they abandoned me under a tree. They walked on for half a day, but couldn't bear the pain of having left me behind. So they turned back and eventually found me. My father later told me that they washed me in a nearby stream, then wrapped me in old clothes. We continued the journey

together. Later, we escaped to Malaysia. About ten years later, we ended up in Hong Kong. When I was still young and living in Malaysia, we used to wait by the coconut trees for the coconut crabs to come down. Their claws were very strong—they could break open the coconut shells. We would catch them and bring them home to mother. Wow! They gave out an aroma of both coconut and crab! Hong Kong doesn't have this kind of crabs. When I make the dish now, I give it a Malaysian twist and call it Malaysian Chilli Crabs. My husband's family loves me—and they love the Malaysian dishes I make. One day, I was in the community centre, chatting with my friends about belachan. They thought it was a new dish in the new Chinese restaurants. But no! It is a Malaysian condiment. When it comes to dessert, besides sesame soup and almond soup, there's Mo-mo Cha-cha, with beans, taro, milk and coconut milk. It's healthy and yummy.

Belachan is made the way shrimp paste is, fermented with salt and tiny silver shrimps, and sun-dried. It is used in fried vegetable dishes.

咖哩蟹

新鮮蟹1000克
洋蔥200克
薑蓉、白醋及菜油各2湯匙
辣椒3茶匙
蒜蓉、胡茜粉、小茴香粉及鹽各
1茶匙
薑黃粉1/2茶匙
白醋及菜油各2湯匙
椰奶400毫升
芫茜數條

1 蟹揭蓋洗淨，斬出蟹鉗，以刀背敲破蟹鉗外殼。蟹身剁成四至六塊（視蟹之大小而定），蟹蓋整個留用
2 燒紅鑊落油，放入洋蔥、蒜蓉、薑蓉、辣椒，炒出香味
3 加入胡茜粉、小茴香粉、薑黃粉、椰奶
4 加入蟹件，中火兜炒6分鐘後*，以醋及鹽調味
5 蟹蓋覆在最面，蓋上鑊蓋，煮焗數分鐘後，待蟹熟即可食用，以芫茜伴碟。

* 加入蟹件兜炒時，動作不要太大，以免蟹肉散開

Chilli Crabs

1kg fresh crab
200 g onions
1 tbsp chopped ginger
3 tsps chilli
1 tsp each chopped garlic, coriander powder, cumin powder and salt
½ tsp tumeric powder
2 tbsps each white vinegar and vegetable oil
400 ml coconut milk
some parsley

1 Separate upper shell and claws from crab. Wash and wipe dry. Crack crab claws with the back of chopping knife.
Cut crab into four to six pieces (depending on size of crab). Set aside upper shell of crab.
2 Heat wok and pour in vegetable oil. Add onions, chilli, chopped garlic and ginger. Stir-fry until fragrant.
3 Add the rest of the ingredients and mix.
4 Add the crab pieces and claws. Stir-fry* on medium heat for six minutes. Add vinegar and salt to taste.
5 Put upper shell of crab on top. Cook for a few minutes with cover on. Garnish with parsley.

** Stir gently after adding the crab so that the meat won't detach.*

麼麼咋咋

三角豆、眉豆、紅豆、
紅腰豆、綠豆及芋頭各40克
西米25克
冰糖175克，椰漿1罐

1 芋頭去皮洗淨切粒，備用
2 所有豆類，用清水浸1小時
3 煮沸4杯水，加入西米，再滾後改成小火，待西米煮至半透明，取出用冷水沖洗，瀝乾備用
4 將6杯水煮沸後，加入所有豆及芋頭粒*，大火煮約5分鐘，然後加入冰糖，用慢火煮至材料熟透
5 加入西米，再滾後，離火
6 加入椰漿，便可食用**

* 烹煮時，可依個人口味加入番薯粒、粟米粒
** 進食時，亦可加入季節性水果，例如：芒果、哈密瓜（切粒），增加口感

Mo-mo Cha-cha

40g each triangular beans, black-eyed beans, red beans, kidney beans, mung beans and taro
25g sago
175g rock sugar
1 tin coconut paste

1 Peel and dice taro. Set aside.
2 Soak all the beans with water for one hour.
3 Bring four cups of water to a boil. Add taro*. After it has reboiled, set to low heat and cook until semi-transparent. Remove from heat and rinse to cool. Drain and set aside.
4 Bring six cups of water to a boil. Add all the beans and diced taro. Cook for about five minutes on high heat. Add rock sugar and cook on low heat.
5 Add sago. After it has reboiled, remove from heat.
6 Finally, add coconut paste, then serve**.

** Diced sweet potato or corn can be added during cooking as preferred.*
*** Seasonal fruit like diced mango and honey dew enhance the taste and texture.*

有一次，兄弟姐妹趁著媽媽不在家，
偷偷跟鄰居去放炮仗……

One day when mother wasn't home,
we all sneaked out with our neighbours and played with firecrackers.

黃彩鸞 六十七歲 祖籍中山

我在澳門出生，在學堂讀書至中二，十二歲左右來港學製衣。在港定居後，跟姑媽住在連私人廁所、廚房也沒有的天台木屋。大小二便都是用痰罐，收集滿一罐後就拿到下一層，倒進一個大木桶裡。有人會來「倒夜香」，哪有現在家家戶戶有獨立廁所那麼方便。可能從小就過得清貧，覺得這也沒什麼大不了。在澳門時，一家住在二樓，七兄弟姐妹打地鋪睡閣樓，爹娘睡在下面，家裡也沒有獨立廚房、廁所及浴室。那時跟叔父一起住，燒飯、如廁甚至洗澡，也要到一樓公用的廚房和廁所，才真的不方便。媽媽是家庭主婦，爸爸在香港工作，一年只回家三、四次，一家人很少機會齊齊整整的。暴動後，一家終於團聚了。由於當時樓價便宜，一呎只要幾百塊，於是我們便買了一個兩房一廳的單位。新居有私家廁所，初時反而有點不習慣呢！童年時，太平盛世，中門大開睡覺也可以，媽媽卻不准我們出外玩，放學就要趕回家。有一次，兄弟姐妹趁著媽媽不在家，偷偷跟鄰居去放炮仗，拿著一大餅的炮仗，挖洞、插引、放炮，非常好玩。我排行第二，有一個大哥。家貧，跟著大哥來港賺錢養家。大哥原為裁縫，後來轉做銀行「後生」。當時請人不太著重學歷，大哥都是跟頭跟尾學起來的。我會車衫，但因年紀小，不能在工廠工作，只好在家中跟姑媽學習做胸圍鈎扣。年紀大一點就與表姐一起到製衣廠工作。我的丈夫是我在製衣廠工作時一位老朋友介紹的，相睇後才開始交往，一年後便結婚。丈夫是台山人，以前曾做汽車燒焊，在馳名造雨傘的梁蘇記打過工，後來在廚房學師，退休前亦當過保安員。婚後我們搬到大角咀住板間房，1982年搬到牛頭角，當時還沒有街市及「Y型」居屋。我們夫妻二人絕對是牛頭角上邨的「開荒牛」。一家四口住在牛頭角樂華邨，對我來說，這簡直是個夢寐以求的地方。第一、交通網絡完善；第二、買東西方便；第三、空氣好，環境舒適。有空時在邨內或附近散步，十分享受，所以暫時不打算再搬遷。我常給女兒煲【黃皮薯仔番茄紅衫魚湯】，因她最喜歡這款湯水。

那時抽水馬桶或坐廁不普及，於是有專人收集各家各戶的便溺，就像今天收集垃圾一樣。因為通常是晚上來收集排洩物的，「夜來臭」就戲說是「夜來香」。清理的人會搖鈴，一聽到搖鈴聲又未將糞桶放置在屋外的話，即使正在吃飯也會立刻放下碗筷，誰都不敢怠慢，一錯過，臭物可就要留在屋裡多一天了。

I was born in Macau. All seven of us slept on the floor and in the attic. My parents slept underneath. We had no kitchen, toilet or bathroom. When we cooked, or needed to go to the toilet or take a shower, we had to go to the public area on the first floor. It was quite a hassle. We would pee in a tin bucket. When one was full, we would take it down to the big wooden bucket on the ground floor. At night, someone

Flush toilets were not popular during those times. Like street cleaners, workers were hired to collect waste. They did so during the night. The workers would ring a bell. Households that had not brought their buckets out would immediately do so, because missing the collection time could mean leaving the smelly business idle for another two days. Nocturnal fragrance, or *ye heung*, is a Cantonese euphemism for excrement.

would come to clear the nocturnal fragrance. My father worked in Hong Kong and came home only three or four times a year. We seldom spent time together as a family. I'm the second oldest of the children, and I have an older brother. Our mother never let us play outside after school. We had to go straight home. One day when mother wasn't home, we all sneaked out with our neighbours and played with firecrackers. Armed with big packs of them, we dug holes, lit the fuses and blew them up. It was so much fun! It was difficult for our family to make ends meet, so when I was about twelve I came to Hong Kong with my older brother, who was a tailor, to find work. I got a job making clothes. We lived with my aunt in a wooden hut on the roof of a building. There was no private toilet or kitchen. We used a spittoon as a toilet and when it was full, we would take it downstairs and pour it into a big wooden bucket. At night, people would come and collect it. But I'd always lived a simple, poor life, so for me that was nothing. My brother later became a youngster [Cantonese colloquial term for a messenger] in a bank. At that time, education wasn't necessary for getting a job. At first, I was too young to work in a factory, so I used to sew at home. I learned from my aunt how to make the buckles for brassieres. When I was a little older, I went to work in a garment factory with my cousin. After the riots in 1967, our family was reunited. Flats were cheap at that time—one square foot cost only a few hundred dollars. So, we bought a flat with two rooms and one living room. My brothers and sisters would sleep in a three-tiered bed in the corridor. And there was a private toilet, something I had to get used to! I met my future husband through a friend when I was working in a garment factory. A year later, we got married. My husband is from Toi Shan. He used to be a welder at a car plant. He has also worked in the Leung So Kei Umbrella Factory, as an apprentice in a kitchen and, before he retired, as a security guard. When we got married, we moved to a small place in Tai Kok Tsui. In 1982, we moved to Ngau Tau Kok. Back then, there was no wet market or housing estates. For me, it's a dream place to live. Transport and shopping are easy, the air is fresh, and the environment is pleasant. When I have time, I like to stroll around the estate or the nearby areas. I enjoy that a lot. I don't intend to move.

黃皮薯仔番茄紅衫魚湯

紅衫魚1斤（用比較細小的，湯較香甜）
薑3片
黃皮薯仔3個
番茄2個
紅蘿蔔1個
清水10杯
鹽、油、胡椒粉適量

1 將紅衫魚洗淨刨鱗，用少許鹽醃好
2 以3片薑、油落鍋煎香紅衫魚
3 3個荷蘭黃皮薯仔刨皮，切成細角
4 加入切成4份的番茄和1個切成5至6塊的紅蘿蔔
5 把煲薯仔的水放至剛煎好的魚中，湯便會變成如牛奶一般的奶白色，然後全放進薯仔煲中煲至軟身
6 滾一個鐘頭便會出味

Golden Thread Fish in Yellow Skin Potato and Tomato Soup

600 g golden thread fish
(smaller fish give a sweeter taste)
3 piece of ginger
3 yellow skin potatoes, from Holland
2 tomatoes
1 carrot
10 cups water
some salt, oil and pepper

1. Scale fish, wash and rinse. Spread fish with a few pinches of salt.
2. Fry ginger and fish in wok until slightly brown.
3. Boil potato. Peel off skin and cut into small chunks. Save the water.
4. Cut tomato into 4 pieces and carrot into 5-6 pieces. Add to potato soup.
5. Pour water from the boiled potato into the wok of fish. After bubbling, the soup becomes milk-white. Add in the rest of ingredients and stew until the potatoes become soft.
6. Keep boiling for about an hour to bring out flavour.

我家是種粟米的，順理成章，
我要幫忙看守粟米田。

My family grew corn, so I guarded the fields.

那不是什麼美食，但已是我的所有。十歲的時候，在新會河塘的鄉下，農家都很窮，小孩子就已經要幫忙工作。我家是種粟米的，順理成章，我要幫忙看守粟米田。在粟米成熟期的兩個月內，更要在田裡日夕看守。當時我矮小，就要攀爬上龍眼樹上站崗，好看清楚整個粟米田有沒有盜賊。最苦是，餐餐也要吃粟米飯。天天從田裡新鮮採下來的粟米，香甜是香甜，只是天天吃就厭了，況且吃得多會很口渴。那時候看見每日放牧回來的牧牛仔，於是靈機一觸，心生一計。有天就叫牧牛仔停下來，拿粟米跟他換牛奶。他走了一整天路累透了，自然樂意之至。他鮮搾下來的水牛奶，暖烘烘，很鮮味，很鮮味。那已是1942年左右的事，還未解放。幾年後我走難到香港，從此以後再沒有喝過那麼鮮美的水牛奶，而今天吃的粟米總沒有以前的「粉軟」。那時，我試著將粟米放進換回來的水牛奶裡一齊吃，發覺兩者原來是上好配搭，自此就創出「粟米牛奶」。今天我改良成【鮮奶粟米雞湯】，以粟米、紅蘿蔔與雞煲湯，最後加入鮮奶，成為又濃又甜的營養湯，家人讚不絕口呢。

中國早年民間多為務農，種植水稻、粟米、蔬菜為主。戰亂禍患之時，有窮人偷取飢農作物充飢，因此農民得找人看守農田。今天中國日趨現代化，大多農田已改作工廠用地。

李漢有　七十八歲　祖籍新會

I grew up in He Tang, which is in Xinhui. The farmers' families were very poor, and even the small children had to help with the work. My family grew corn, so I guarded the fields. Two months before harvest, I would stand watch from day to night. I was about ten, but I was short and small, so I had to climb up a tall longan tree to look out for thieves. The hardest

part was having to eat corn-kernel rice every day. The corn we got from the field was sweet, but I got bored eating it every day. Also, eating too much makes you thirsty. The boys who looked after the buffaloes used to walk past the fields every day, so I stopped one and asked him to exchange milk for some corn. He was happy to do so. The milk was fresh and warm. That was in 1942, before the war and before liberation. A few years later, when the war began, we fled to Hong Kong. I've never had such fresh milk again. And the corn we get nowadays isn't as soft and sweet as it was back then. I used to put the corn into the milk and eat them together. I realised they were a good match. That's how I came up with this Milky Chicken Corn Soup by adding carrots and chicken. Put the milk in last. It becomes a nutritious, sweet and thick soup. My family loves it.

Li Sin Yau 78 years old Hometown Xinhui

芋頭鯪魚腐皮卷

芋頭300克
鯪魚肉120克
紹興酒2茶匙
糖1/2茶匙，鹽1/4茶匙
糖、鹽、胡椒粉、麻油少許
腐皮1張
唐芹菜或韭黃1棵（切段）
薑1-2片
芡汁：麻油少許，蠔油1湯匙，生粉1茶匙

1 芋頭去皮，切粗條後，起鑊加入鹽(1/4茶匙)、糖(1/4茶匙)、紹興酒(2茶匙)、薑片，一同爆香，煮至八成熟便可，取出備用
2 鯪魚肉加入少許糖、鹽、胡椒粉、麻油，拌勻，攪至起膠，煎熟後，切粗條
3 圓形腐皮，用乾布抹拭後，剪裁成12塊正方形小腐皮
4 將芋頭條、鯪魚肉條、唐芹菜或韭黃放在小腐皮上，包成春卷形，用少許生粉開水，黏口
5 慢火煎腐皮卷至四面金黃，然後隔水蒸15分鐘
6 蠔油、糖、麻油、生粉開水煮成芡汁，澆在腐皮卷上，便可食用

Bean Curd Roll with Taro and Minced Dace

300 g taro
120 g minced dace
2 tsp Shaoxing wine
½ tsp sugar
¼ tsp salt
sugar, salt, pepper and sesame oil to taste
one soya bean sheet
1 stalk Chinese celery or chives, cut into pieces
1 – 2 slices ginger
sauce : sugar and sesame oil to taste, 1 tbsp oil, 1 tsp cornstarch

1 Remove taro skin and cut taro into thick sticks. Heat wok with oil, add in seasoning for taro plus ginger slices. Fry taro until about 80% cooked or until soft.
2 Season minced dace with sugar, salt, pepper and sesame oil, mix well and stir until it reaches a glutinous consistency. Fry the mince dace flat on both sides, then cut into sticks.
3 Wipe the bean curd sheet with a dry cloth and cut into 12 squares.
4 Place one taro stick, one fish stick and a piece of celery or chive onto each square. Roll into a spring roll and seal the rolls with a cornstarch mixture (1 tsp cornstarch + 1½ tbsp cold water).
5 Slowly fry the bean curd rolls until golden brown, then steam on high heat for 15 minutes.
6 Mix the sauce with ⅓ bowl of cold water. Bring to a boil in the wok and pour over the bean curd rolls. Serve immediately.

鮮奶粟米雞湯

雞1隻
粟米2條
紅蘿蔔1個
薑3片
鮮奶1杯

1 雞洗淨，去皮、氽水後過冷河，瀝乾水分
2 紅蘿蔔去皮切大塊，洗淨備用
3 粟米切開數段，洗淨備用
4 煲滾一鍋水，放入雞、紅蘿蔔、粟米、薑*
5 再滾起時，改用慢火煲兩小時
6 加入鮮奶，再度滾起後**，加鹽調味即可飲用

* 如加入瘦肉，湯水就更鮮甜
** 為免營養流失，鮮奶不可久滾

Milky Chicken Corn Soup

1 whole chicken (2kg)
2 cobs fresh corn
1 carrot
3 slices ginger
1 cup fresh milk

1 Clean chicken. Skin, blanch and rinse under tap water. Dry.
2 Peel carrot and cut into large pieces. Wash and set aside.
3 Cut corn into several sections. Wash and set aside.
4 Bring one pot of water to a boil. Put in chicken, carrot, corn and ginger.*
5 Reboil on a low heat and cook for two hours.
6 Add the milk. Reboil on a low heat. Add salt to taste.

Include some lean pork to enhance the flavour of the soup.

詩詞歷史我滾瓜爛熟！

I am brilliant in poetry and history!

李繼唐 終年七十七歲 祖籍中山

我曾任公務員，熱愛藝術，退休後就前往廣州美術學院進修。之後，更於廣東畫院舉辦水磨及信義宗神學院畫展。從1997年起，我一有空就於各教會或老人院當義工，教授書法、國畫及太極劍。在家中會聽聽音樂，心血來潮時還會拉拉小提琴，自我陶醉一番。不得不提的是，我對中國文學和文化的研究，詩詞歷史當然滾瓜爛熟，有時候，我還會在一些宗教雜誌裡面寫專欄文章呢！現在，大概就是這樣享受我多年來培養的藝術生活。私下，我尚有很多興趣，其中最愛吃。飲早茶，吃點心，賞心樂事。除了中國菜，亦十分愛吃牛排和海鮮。年幼時不太喜歡吃雞，只鍾情牛和豬，直至有一次，爸爸弄了一個【缽頭雞】，試過後對吃雞的態度就有一百八十度的改變。雞從此成為我最愛的食品之一。後來，還常常跟爸爸一起弄缽頭雞。回想起來，仍歷歷在目。

缽，梵文pàtra，指僧人盛載飯食的器具，泛指盛酒、裝東西的圓形金屬或陶瓷用具。廣東小吃「砵仔糕」，傳統的製法就是以黃糖、粘米粉等放在一個瓦製的小砵內蒸熟。

Li Kai Tong 77 years old (deceased) Hometown Zhongshan

I'm now retired. I love literature and art and was enrolled in an arts programme in Guangzhou. I even showed some of my work at exhibitions there—that was about ten or fifteen years ago. Sometimes I work as a volunteer at the church and in homes for the elderly. I teach them calligraphy, painting and *tai chi*. I also play the violin, and sometimes contribute to the church journal. I enjoy *yum cha*. It's one of the most enjoyable experiences in life. I also like seafood and steak. When I was young, I used to eat only pork and beef because I didn't like chicken. But one day my father made a dish called Earthen Bowl Chicken and I changed my mind! He put chicken, wine, soy sauce and oil in a bowl, and he covered it with wet steaming paper. After a while, the paper would harden, which meant that the chicken was ready. It was so delicious! My father taught me how to make it. Now, chicken is my favourite dish.

The earthen bowl is widely used in Guangdong cooking. A snack called Earthen Bowl Pudding is traditionally made with flour and brown sugar and steamed.

缽頭雞

雞半隻（約450克）
醃料：麻油、碎冰糖各1湯匙，
米酒半杯，老抽、頭抽各2湯匙，
蒜3瓣（剁蓉），薑2厚片（剁蓉）

1 雞洗淨，瀝乾水分，斬件，
  下醃料拌勻，醃約20分鐘
2 將雞件排放瓦缽內
3 以沙紙*或牛油紙蓋著瓦缽
4 沿著瓦缽邊緊按紙張，並以橡筋
  或繩固定位置，密封好
5 水滾後下鍋，隔水蒸約18分鐘
6 取出後**，以薑蔥作點綴即可食用

* 蒸煮食物的沙紙可於「紙紮鋪」購買
** 打開沙紙時，小心蒸氣燙手

Earthen Bowl Chicken

450 g chicken
marinade : 1 tbsp each sesame oil and crushed rock sugar, ½ cup Chinese rice wine, 2 tbsp each dark soy sauce and premium soy sauce, 3 cloves garlic (minced), 2 thick slices ginger (minced)

1 Wash chicken, wipe dry and cut into pieces. Marinate for 20 minutes.
2 Place chicken pieces neatly into casserole dish.
3 Cover earthen bowl with steaming paper.* Make sure the paper is pressed firmly around the rim of the casserole dish and use rubber bands or string to keep it tightly in place.
4 Boil water in a steaming pot, put casserole dish inside and steam for about 18 minutes.
5 Remove casserole dish and unwrap steaming paper**. Garnish with spring onions and shredded ginger to serve.

** This paper for Chinese steamed and stew dishes can be found in the stores that sell paper money for the dead and lanterns for festivals.*
*** Be careful of the hot steam when unwrapping the paper.*

我現在仍然保存以前穿的大襟衫。

I still have my Chinese nanny's outfit:
a snow-white top and black silk pants. It's a status symbol.

梁崇　八十二歲　祖籍西樵

我十多歲就在家人安排下許配了人。但拜堂那天，我就逃了出來，決定自食其力，自此加入了聞名的「自梳女」行列。初時，我到香港的大戶人家做雜工，後來就照顧小少爺，學煮飯。以前伙頭煮飯，我也在旁偷師，什麼【粒粒炒豆角】、焗乳鴿等廣東名菜都一一學會，湯水當然樣樣精。我「一腳踢」什麼都做，由於家主、家母都是專業人士，對僕人非常的友善。就這樣，半生就過了。幾年前退休，在觀塘買了一間姑婆屋和姊妹一起住，不過有空仍常到戶主家做這做那，其實，他們都已變成我的家人了。上教會，返團契，都在一起的。我現在仍然保存以前穿的大襟衫：雪白色的上衣與黑綢褲。那是身分的象徵，不是很多人能穿成這樣的，當然還有頸後那一條粗黑的大辮。

梳起不嫁的婦女俗稱「自梳女」。宣告梳起發誓永世不嫁，要擇定吉日，宴請親朋，向神靈和祖宗牌位稟告。梳起不嫁通常一是因為家貧要留家幫忙，二是反抗父母安排的婚姻或意中人變心，三是家有世代相傳的當家姑婆之規。

My family arranged my marriage not long after I turned ten. But on the day of the wedding, I ran away and decided to become a *zi shu nu* sister. I worked for a big, wealthy family in Hong Kong and learned how to cook and take care of children. When the chef was cooking, I would watch. I learned how to make green bean, baked pigeon and many other

well-known Cantonese dishes. My employers were very friendly. That's how I spent half of my life. I retired several years ago and bought an apartment in Kwun Tong where I live with my sisters. When I have time, I still go back to help at my old employers' home. I've become part of the family. We even go to church together. I still have my Chinese nanny's outfit: a snow-white top and black silk pants. It's a status symbol.

Literally, *zi shu nu* means women who comb up their hair. It refers to women who decide to remain single. Women may do this for various reasons: to stay home to help their poor family, to object against an arranged marriage, to follow the rule in some families that a woman be the head of the household...

粒粒炒豆角

青豆角80克
叉燒60克
馬蹄8-10粒
豆乾4塊*
西芹2條
紅蘿蔔半條
薑蓉及蒜蓉各1湯匙
調味：鹽、糖各半茶匙

1 將材料切粒備用
2 燒熱鍋，下青豆角粒，炒片刻後下少許油，加薑蓉、蒜蓉同炒
3 加入1至2湯匙水，蓋上蓋，煮一煮
4 下其他材料一同炒香，加入調味炒勻，便可食用**

* 亦可用大頭菜代替豆乾，較香口及惹味
**食用時可灑上花生，吃起來較有嚼頭

Fried Diced String Bean Mix

80 g green string beans
60 g roast pork
8 - 10 pieces water chestnuts
4 pieces preserved bean curd*
2 stalks celery
half stalk carrot
1 tbsp each crushed ginger and garlic
seasoning : ½ tsp each salt and sugar

1 Dice all ingredients and set aside.
2 Heat wok and stir fry the green string beans awhile. Add a little oil and fry quickly together with crushed ginger and garlic.
3 Add 1-2 tbsp of water. Cook with cover on for a little while.
4 Put in the rest of ingredients and stir fry; add in seasonings, fry briefly and serve. Sprinkle with peanuts for a crunchy bite.

* *Using pickled vegetables instead of preserved bean curd gives a fuller taste.*

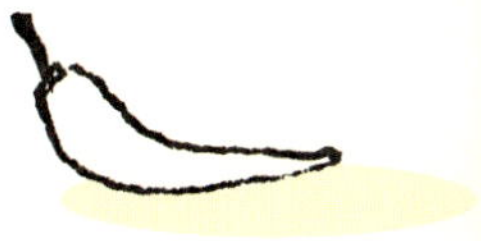

婆婆女書
I AM

在我的家庭，只有男生才有機會上學。

Only the boys in my family went to school.

王玉英 祖籍廣西海防

最愛吃鹹菜炒墨魚、粉絲炒豆乾、芹菜、【白蘿蔔炆棋子肉】（即切成四方形的肥豬肉，因其形狀似一顆棋子），還有白欖蒸魚。這些地道菜全部都很開胃可口。平常每星期到墟去買魚和肉。過時過節，便有機會吃自己養的雞和豬！味道真的有別於從街市購入的肉類食物，是特別鮮甜。一頭豬可分給鄰居和鄉里共享。農曆新年，我們還會自製「粉利」(即年糕，粉利取意「順順利利」）。每個粉利上，會用八角印上星的形狀。在我的家庭，只有男生才有機會上學。爸爸是賣絲綢的，家裡也有飼養家禽家畜，可以說是自給自足。我是長女，共有十三個弟妹，所以要幫忙煮飯和照顧弟妹。我十二三歲時，日軍入侵，幸好沒有打進我們的村裡，但我常常聽見飛機和爆炸的聲音。當時母親剛去了越南，無法回來，我只好帶著弟妹逃亡。為了逃避炮火，我們走到一片香蕉園去躲避，用蕉葉作遮掩，結果我們都安全避過。在鄉下，仍然有盲婚啞嫁。我本來許配給鄉下一位男子，但由於局勢混亂，母親賠了錢讓我跟那男子悔婚，後來再給我介紹了現在的丈夫。當時他在廣州，我嫁雞隨雞，嫁狗隨狗，一直跟他來到香港。從那時起，我便學習照顧兒女，做半職的家庭主婦。現在連兒孫都長大了，我也有機會去學習。從前沒有機會上學，現在終於有機會學寫大字、跳舞，多采多姿。【紅皮扣肉】是傳統的地道餸菜，大時大節必不可少。由於炸了的豬皮好像燒豬一樣，意頭很好，又好吃，亦夠大方得體，所以這道菜比雞還重要呢！通常酒席完畢，每人也要帶一點回家。

中國傳統婚姻嫁娶需按照三書六禮的習俗。三書即聘書（訂親之書）、禮書（過禮之書，禮物清單）、迎書（迎娶之書，結婚當天接新娘用）。六禮則指婚禮前納采、問名、納吉、納徵、請期、迎親。多講求門當戶對，所謂「竹門對竹門」，要求雙方家庭身分地位合宜對等。由媒人說親，婚事過程由父母全權包辦，「父母之命、媒妁之言」十分重要。有時新郎新娘在婚禮前並不認識對方，是為「盲婚啞嫁」。

I love squid with preserved vegetables, dry bean curd with vermicelli, Chess Pork with Turnip [pork fat cut into squares, like on a chessboard], and steamed fish with Chinese olives. These authentic local dishes are all delicious! I used to buy my fish and meat from the market once a week. During festivals, we would eat chicken and pig from our farm. They taste

so much better than what you get from the market. They're fresh and sweet. One pig can be shared among many neighbours. During Chinese New Year, we used to make *fun li* [New Year Pudding—*li* puns with and sounds like "smoothness"]. We would stamp a star on every *fun li* with a star anise. Only the boys in my family went to school. My father was in silk trading, and we also kept livestock at home. We were more or less self-sufficient. Since I was the eldest, and there were thirteen of us, I used to help with cooking and taking care of my brothers and sisters. When I was twelve or thirteen, the Japanese occupation began. We were lucky they didn't invade our village. But we often heard the sounds of airplanes and bombing. My mother was in Vietnam at the time and couldn't get back. To seek shelter from the bombs, I used to take my brothers and sisters into the banana fields. In my hometown, blind marriages were common. I was meant to marry a man from my hometown, but because of the war, my mother paid compensation to terminate the agreement. Later, I was introduced to my future husband, who came from Guangzhou. In Chinese we say, "Follow a chicken when you marry a chicken; follow a dog when you marry a dog". So I came to Hong Kong with him. From then on, I became a part-time housewife and learned how to take care of our children. Now that my children and grandchildren are all grown up, I have had the chance to study. For years, I didn't have the opportunity to go to school, but now I'm learning to write and even dance. How wonderful! Deep-fried Pig's Skin is an authentic local dish. It's like roast pig. It's a must for any major festival or special occasion. It's auspicious and delicious and more important than chicken. After a banquet, everyone takes a little bit home with them.

Many brides and grooms never met before the marriage, hence the phrase blind marriage. Traditional marriages were determined by the parents of the bride and groom. A marriage was best when "the doors matched", that is, the two families had similar social status. A match-maker would propose a match to the parents, whose decision was final.

紅皮扣肉

五花腩600克
大頭菜一塊（約40克）
芋頭一個（中）
南乳4磚
蜜糖及老抽適量
油4杯
清水2杯

1 洗淨五花腩，以熱水燙至半熟後，用冷水浸30分鐘
2 用叉插五花腩的皮，使皮和肉鬆軟些*
3 塗老抽和蜜糖在五花腩的表面，下油鑊炸香表皮，炸後再浸冷水
4 將炸好的腩肉切厚片，備用
5 芋頭切厚塊，大小如腩肉般，同樣炸至金黃色
6 將芋頭和五花腩一塊塊相間排列，放在容器內
7 大頭菜切粒，與南乳混在一起，加少許水，淋在腩肉芋頭上
8 隔水蒸至少兩個小時，至肉和芋頭燜腍為止

* 肉鬆針處理，以便在油炸時起花

Pork Belly with Taro in Fermented Red Bean Curd

600 g marbled pork belly
40 g mustard cabbage
1 taro (medium-size)
4 pieces of fermented red bean curd
some honey and dark soy sauce
4 cups fried oil
2 cups water

1 Rinse pork belly. Blanch with hot water until it's half-cooked. Immerse in cold water for 30 minutes.
2 Pierce the pork* with a fork to loosen.
3 Coat the pork belly with dark soy sauce and honey, then deep-fry Immerse the meat in cold water.
4 Cut the deep-fried meat and taro into thick slices.
5 Deep-fry the taro slices until golden yellow.
6 Place the slices of meat and taro between one another on a dish.
7 Dice mustard cabbage and mix well with fermented red bean curd. Put the mixture on top of the pork belly and taro.
8 Steam over water for at least two hours, until pork belly and taro become loose and soft.

** Piercing the pork belly also prevents oil from spitting during deep-frying.*

白蘿蔔燜棋子肉

五花腩600克
白蘿蔔300克
大蒜2條（切段）
中國芹菜2條
上湯、清水各1/2杯
薑2片
蒜蓉2茶匙
醃料：鹽、糖、豉油各少許

1 白蘿蔔去皮切大塊，洗淨備用
2 五花腩*洗淨，汆水過冷河，瀝乾水分，切成約1吋x1吋之粗粒（棋子肉）、鹽、糖、豉油醃味備用
3 清水煮沸，加入上湯、蘿蔔、大蒜、芹菜及各種調味，中火煮約10分鐘
4 放棋子肉，中至大火燜約10分鐘

* 可用腩排代替五花腩

Stewed Turnip with Pork Belly

600 g pork belly*, half fat / half lean
300 g turnip
2 stalks each garlic and Chinese celery
1/2 cup each clear broth and water
2 slices ginger
2 tsp chopped garlic
seasoning : some pepper, light and dark soy sauce, sugar & cornstarch

1 Peel turnip. Wash and cut into big chunks.
2 Rinse pork belly, blanch and run under tap water. Drain, wipe dry and cut into one-inch cubes.
3 Marinade pork with seasonings and set aside for 10-15 minutes.
4 Heat wok with oil. Stir-fry ginger slices until fragrant. Add in pork, fry quickly a few times, then add in turnip. Mix well. Add in water and clear broth and bring to a boil. Turn to medium heat and cook for 15 minutes. Turn to low heat and cook for 30 minutes until pork is tender and turnip is cooked.
5 When sauce thickens, sprinkle a few dashes of sesame oil and serve.

** Pork rib belly can be substituted for pork belly.*

……就在那時決定「梳起不嫁」。

That's when I decided to 'comb up my hair'
and never get married.

陸楮　八十七歲　祖籍三水

小時候會吃什麼？種什麼便吃什麼吧！都是瓜瓜菜菜而已。家中雖有七兄弟姐妹，但從沒有爭食！絕對沒有！我們在鄉下三水種瓜種菜，自己吃之外，剩下來的還會拿去賣呢！家中缺錢時，我就當過一些驚險的工作。那時候，家鄉很流行種煙絲，村中的小朋友便被看中運送鴉片。尚未懂事的我便帶著鴉片，運到大沙。那時不知道這是犯法的，不過掙回來的錢總算解決了燃眉之急。當時可沒想過危險，無錢，就無得食，無辦法啦！後來打仗，我便走難到廣州學織布，就在那時決定「梳起不嫁」（見梁崇故事的註）。到了1945年，織布廠搬到香港，我便到香港定居，打過住家工，主要是照顧小孩子。但從來沒有弄些什麼小菜給他們吃，因我不懂燒飯啊！我八十七歲了，尚算十分精壯，中氣十足。現在一個人住，每天吃的都是簡單易煮的菜。對食物的要求不高，有【青紅蘿蔔湯】，便已經很滿足快樂了。

紡織及製衣業是早期香港經濟發展的重要支柱。自四十年代末來港的新移民，大都在工廠工作，又或在家散件加工，為香港的工業發展起著關鍵作用。

What did we eat when we were young? Whatever grew in the fields—mostly leafy vegetables and gourds. I had seven brothers and sisters. Did we fight for food? Never! Our land in Sanshui was so fertile we even had surplus produce to sell at the market. But, whenever the family was short of cash, I would join other children and smuggle opium leaves. We

even went as far as Daisha. I didn't know it was illegal, let alone the risk and danger involved. But it was our only option when we ran out of money. During the war, I went to Guangzhou and learned how to weave. That's when I decided to "comb up my hair" and never get married. In 1945, the weaving factory I worked in moved to Hong Kong, so I went along. But soon, I left the factory to work as a maid for a family and spent most of my time taking care of the children. I didn't know much about cooking. I live by myself now, and make simple, easy dishes. Carrot and Green Turnip Soup makes me happy.

Weaving and garment workers were two pillars of Hong Kong's economic and industrial development in the mid to late 1900s. Many Mainland Chinese moved to Hong Kong in the late 1940s and worked in factories and at home.

青紅蘿蔔湯

青蘿蔔1個
紅蘿蔔2個
煲湯瘦肉或豬肉1條
水10杯
蜜棗3粒

1 青紅蘿蔔洗淨，切大粒
2 瘦肉洗淨，汆水備用
3 蜜棗洗淨待用
4 放入所有材料*，用大火煲至大滾
5 水滾後收至慢火，煲約2小時，加鹽調味即成

* 如想湯更鮮甜，可加入上湯同煲

Carrot and Green Turnip Soup

1 green turnip
2 carrots
300 g lean pork or pork tenderloin
10 cups of water
3 sweet dates

1 Peel and wash green turnip and carrots. Cut into big chunks.
2 Rinse lean pork, blanch and set aside.
3 Rinse sweet dates and set aside.
4 Put all the ingredients in a stock pot.* Bring to a boil on a high heat.
5 After water boils, reset to low heat and cook for about two hours. Add salt to taste.

* *Clear broth can be added to enhance the sweetness of the soup.*

同鄉稱我為「自由女」。

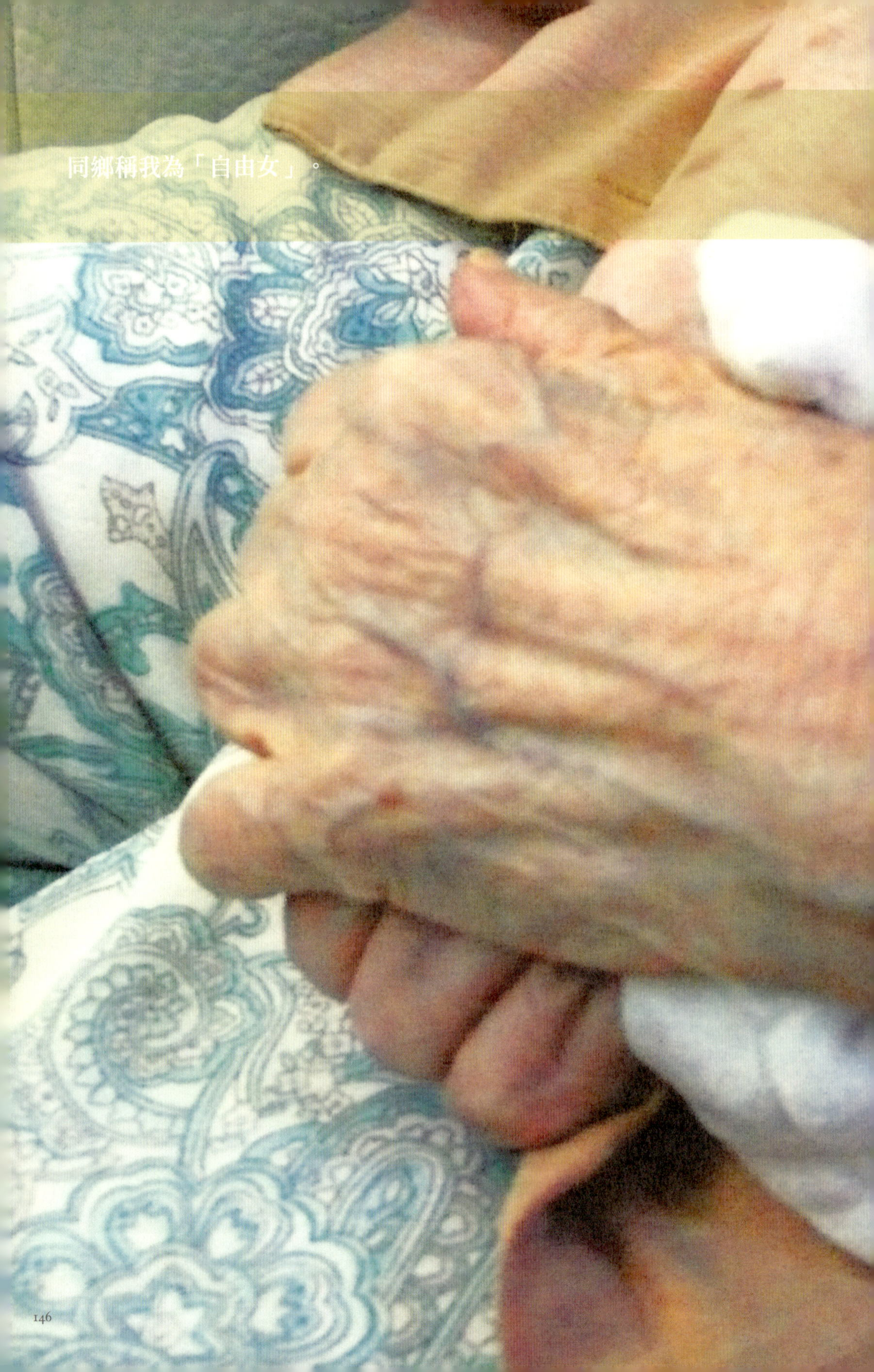

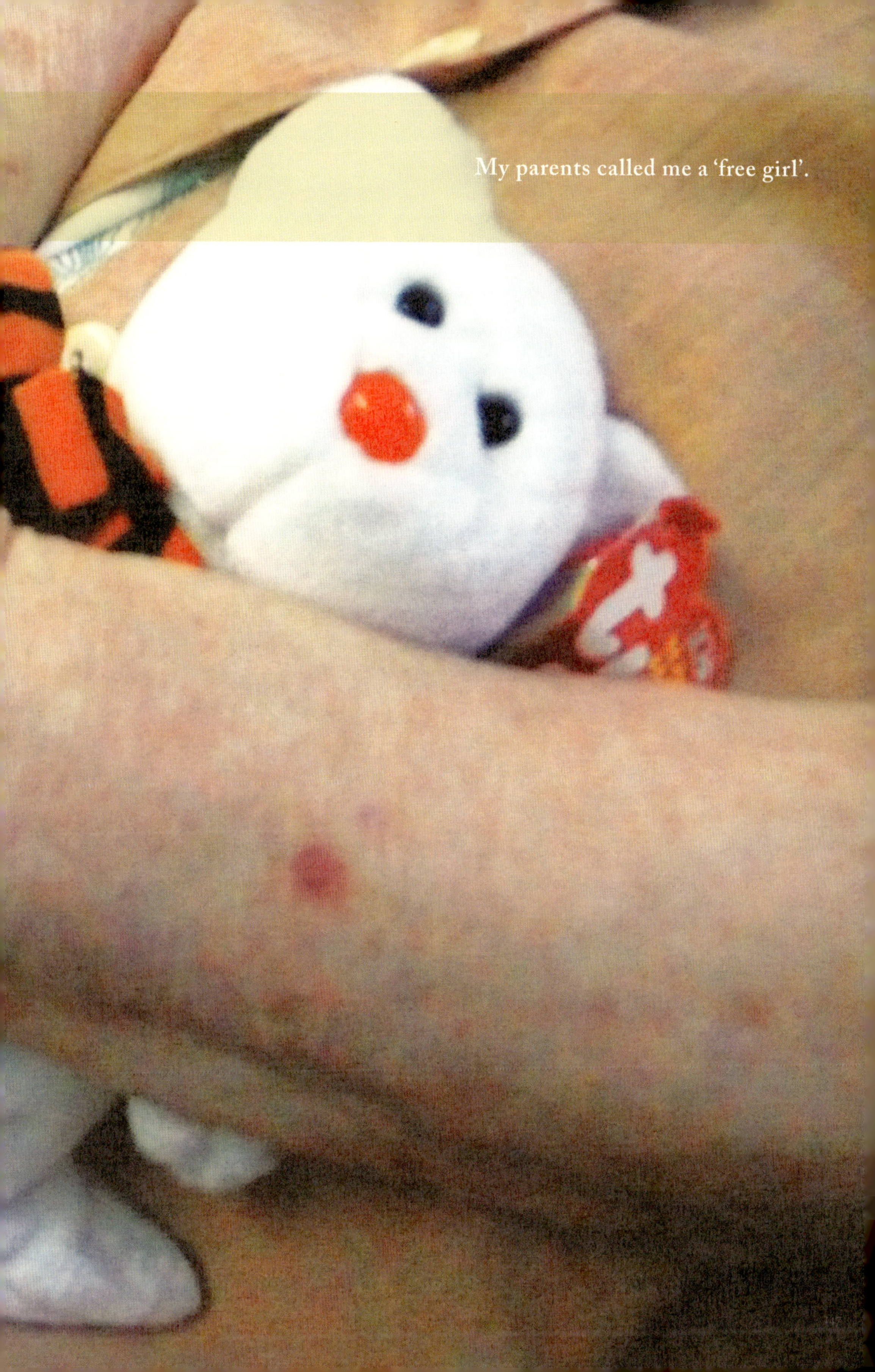

My parents called me a 'free girl'.

梁黃堅心 九十七歲 祖籍寶安

少年時我家婢僕多達三十多人呢。早年到香港求學，受西方教育，就被同鄉稱為「自由女」。中學畢業後，為著理想，入讀護士學校，及後北上廣州醫院學習公共衛生。中日抗戰時，認識了丈夫，一同逃難至西北、重慶等地。為要建設新中國，走遍中國大江南北，四個孩子也相繼出生。在貧困的日子，我曾擺地攤變賣家當呢。解放後移居香港，在醫院工作至退休。從小就不踏足廚房，所以我今年九十七歲了，仍不太懂煮飯。最喜歡吃的是新鮮出爐的軟麵包和糕點；新鮮的、脆脆的「油炸鬼」也不錯。閒時會嘆上一杯香濃的牛奶咖啡……如遇上美味的雪糕更能一口氣吃上三個雪糕球！雪糕可是與兒時友伴一起炮製的美食。一個製雪糕的木桶，內放錫桶，把材料攪呀攪，放點冰塊，放點鹽，是大熱天時的最佳消遣。有得吃，有得玩，不亦樂乎！

木桶有存溫保味、促進發酵的功效。長年久用的木桶所製作的食品，別有一番風味。

A wooden bucket is a good temperature and taste controller. It can also enhance the process of yeasting.

My family was wealthy and we had more than thirty servants. My parents called me a "free girl" because I was educated in Hong Kong. I finished secondary school here, then went to Guangdong to train as a nurse. I met my husband during the war and we fled to Chongqing in the west. We wanted to contribute to the revolutionary effort. My four children were born during this time. After the liberation, we came to Hong Kong, and I worked in a hospital until I retired. I never spent much time in the kitchen. I don't think I can even make a proper meal. But I enjoy coffee, freshly baked pastries and fried dough. I love ice-cream as well! And I know how to make it at home! It's so much fun stirring and blending the ingredients in a wooden bucket, then adding ice and salt. It's so good in the summer.

芒果雪糕

芒果蓉1杯
淡忌廉1杯
煉奶1/3杯

1 將淡忌廉打至8分企身
2 加入煉奶、芒果蓉，拌勻
3 放入冰箱約45分鐘，至雪糕漿面稍呈雪霜狀為合
4 用叉子撥打雪糕漿至略為鬆散，再放回冰箱
5 重複步驟3及4一至兩次後，再冷藏6小時便成

食用前把雪糕放回室溫約5分鐘，口感更佳。配新鮮芒果粒同吃，更能帶出雪糕的奶味

Mango Ice Cream

1 cup mashed mango
1 cup light cream
1/3 cup condensed milk

1 Whip light cream until stiff.
2 Add condensed milk and mango. Mix well.
3 Chill in freezer for about 45 minutes until the top becomes frosty.
4 Loosen the ice cream with a fork, then return to freezer.
5 Repeat once or twice. Chill in freezer for a further six hours. Serve with fresh diced mango to bring out the milky flavour.

To give the ice cream a fine, smooth texture, leave it out at room temperature for about five minutes before serving. Serve with fresh mango to bring out the taste of milk in the ice-cream.

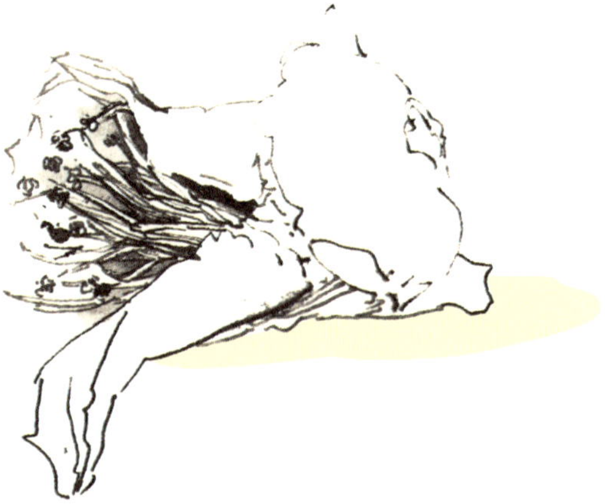

邊做邊學

I LEARN

我是唸護士的，曾是一位校醫。

I got a job as a nurse at a school in Fujian.

劉秀華　八十五歲　祖籍福州

我來香港定居的時候是1984年5月，算算指頭，已有二十多年了。來港以前，在福建居住了一段很長時間。我是唸護士的，曾是一位校醫。我有兩個弟弟和兩個妹妹，父親是手藝技工，那就是你們說的裁縫了。雖然家境貧窮，但慶幸自己還有讀書的機會。小學和初中的時候，我是一位工讀生。那時的學校，如果讀書成績好，到中學的時候就連伙食費也可以不用交。以前唸護士、師範這一類職業學校都不用付學費，因為學費和伙食都可以從工資裡扣除。還記得學校的規矩很嚴，學護都要為病人量體溫和整理床舖。如果學護不小心摔破了體溫表或弄壞了其他器具，我們要在畢業後多留幾天，以額外的工作來補償。要不是因為有學費減免，我想我是不會選讀護士的，因為我從小就怕鬼，晚上不敢自己一個人睡。1950年，我被調到學校做校醫，並認識了當時當教師的丈夫。後來丈夫去世，一個人帶著五個孩子，繼續當校醫直到退休。雖然那時候生活很苦，但比上不足，比下有餘。我的孩子都很勤力，有些大學畢業，有些中學畢業，每一個都有唸書，感謝上帝！人最重要的就是過得快樂，若知道別人有困難，能幫得上忙就應該去幫，能做得到的就去做。說到吃，要數當學護期間和同學一起做的簡單小吃【蠔煎】。材料很簡單，也很好吃。不過，我得意之作還是【鍋邊糊】，拿過烹飪比賽亞軍呢。另一就是我福州鄉下的過年食物【雞腸麵】。

「蠔煎」也稱「蠔仔煎」、「蠔仔烙」，是源自潮州的特色小吃。煎得好的蠔煎，一面是晶瑩的番薯粉，一面是金黃色的煎蛋，兩面微焦，蠔仔粒夾在中間，似有若無卻個個飽滿，外鬆脆清香，內韌滑鮮甜。

I came to Hong Kong in May, 1984. It's been over twenty years. Before that, I lived in Fuzhou. I went to nursing school and I was working as a physician at a school. I have two younger brothers and two younger sisters. My father was a tailor. Although we were poor, I was lucky that I could go to school, but I also had to work all through primary and junior secondary

school. In those days, if students did well, they got a free education and even free meals and board at school. It was also free to study at vocational schools because they would deduct the fees and the cost of your food from your salary. The school rules were very strict. Among other things, student nurses had to check patients' temperatures and make their beds. If you broke a thermometer or any other equipment, you had to spend a few more days working after graduation to compensate for it. If school hadn't been free, I never would have chosen to become a nurse. That's because I've always been afraid of ghosts—even now, I'm afraid of sleeping alone at night. In 1950, I got a job as a nurse at a school in Fujian. My future husband was a teacher there. We had five children. After he died, life was often very difficult—but there's always someone worse off than you. I stayed on at the school until I retired. My children are very hard-working and some of them went to university. It's so important to live happily. The snacks I used to have with my friends at nursing school were the most memorable—like pan-fried oysters. The ingredients are simple, but it's delicious. The dish I make is Pot-Rim Rice Paste. I won second-runner-up in a cooking contest with it. There's also a New Year delicacy in my hometown called "Chicken Intestines" in Soup.

This dish originates from Chaozhou in Guangdong. Good pan-fried oysters have sweet potato paste on one side and eggs on the other. Both sides are a little brown, with oysters smooth and sweet in the inside.

雞腸麵

地瓜粉（番薯粉）75克
蛋1隻
水200克
鹽少許
蔥花適量

1 混合地瓜粉和鹽
2 蛋與水攪勻
3 將蛋液逐少倒入地瓜粉內，混合成糊漿，待用
4 加入蔥花，燒熱平底鑊，放入適量糊漿，慢火煎成薄餅皮*
5 待薄餅皮冷後，切成幼條，便是雞腸麵條
6 可用清湯或加入其他材料，煮成雞腸湯麵

* 煎薄餅皮時，要注意厚薄平均

"Chicken Intestines" in Soup (Pancake Shreds in Clear Broth)

75 g potato starch
1 egg
200 g water
some salt
some chopped spring onions

1 Mix and sift potato starch and salt.
2 Whisk egg with water.
3 Add egg mixture to potato starch, little by little. Mix into a paste. Set aside.
4 Use a low heat. Put chopped spring onions into a heated flat-bottom pan. Put in an appropriate amount of flour paste* to make a pancake.
5 When the pancake cools, cut into thin shreds (resembling chicken intestines).
6 Boil the pancake shreds and any other ingredients in clear broth or other soup base.

* *Make sure the paste is evenly spread out.*

蠔煎(蚵仔煎)

蠔仔300克
地瓜粉1/2杯
蔥、蒜及鹽適量
清水少許

1 用少許鹽將蠔仔洗淨
2 洗淨蔥、蒜，切小粒備用
3 蠔仔、地瓜粉和蔥、蒜攪拌成糊狀，放少許鹽
4 燒熱油鍋倒下糊漿。慢火煎熟至金黃色即可*

* 吃時可放少許胡椒粉或蘸魚露

Pan-fried Oysters

300 g small to medium-size oysters
½ cup potato flour
some spring onions and garlic
some oil, salt and water
a pinch of pepper
some fish sauce

1 Clean and rinse oysters with salt.
2 Finely chop spring onions and garlic. Set aside.
3 Mix oysters, potato flour, spring onions and garlic. Stir into a paste. Add a few pinches of salt.
4 Heat oil in a wok. Pan-fry oyster paste on a low heat until golden brown. Serve with a few pinches of pepper and fish sauce to taste.

鍋邊糊

米2杯
清湯或雞湯約1杯
水約6杯
瘦肉、冬菇絲、紅蘿蔔絲及紫菜適量

1 米洗淨後，用清水浸過夜
2 將米撈出瀝乾水，放攪拌機內，加入約1500克的水，攪成米漿
3 將清湯加約1倍水倒進中式鑊內煮沸
4 在清湯之水平線上，沿鑊之圓周塗抹一層油
5 用碗舀米漿*，沿著鑊之圓周繞一圈，倒出米漿
6 蓋上蓋，煮約半分鐘
7 打開蓋，將鑊邊的熟米漿片鏟到湯裡，煮至熟透後，撈出備用
8 再加添清湯和水，待沸後，重複上述步驟，直至米漿做完為止
9 可按個人口味加入紫菜、瘦肉等材料與湯同煮，跟著放入熟米漿片煮一會，便成「鍋邊糊」了

* 舀米漿時，記得要將米漿略攪拌

Pot-rim Rice Paste

2 cups white rice
1 cup clear broth or chicken broth
6 cups water
some shredded winter mushrooms, carrots, seaweed and lean pork

1 Rinse rice and soak overnight with water.
2 Strain rice and put into blender. Add about 3 cups of water and blend into a paste.
3 Pour half of the clear broth into a wok. Add same amount of water and bring to a boil.
4 Spread oil along inner ring of wok, just above the water level.
5 Measure one rice bowl of rice paste. Stir while pouring it around the oiled upper rim of the wok.
6 Cook for 30 seconds with cover on.
7 Scrape the cooked rice paste into the broth. When soft, remove, drain and set aside.
8 Add the rest of the clear broth and water to the wok, as above. Repeat until all the rice paste is used up.
9 Cook seaweed and lean pork in the broth. Add the cooked rice paste pieces and cook for a little while. Serve.

我十二歲左右便來了香港做裁縫學徒。

When I was twelve,
I came to Hong Kong to be a tailor's apprentice.

梁紹錦　八十九歲　祖籍恩平

兒時最喜愛吃鹹魚、蝦籽柚皮和【蒸粉果】。粉果的材料有蝦米、花生、蔥和豬肉碎，材料煮熟後可以存放一段長時間，所以家裡常常吃，也成為了家常菜。每逢過時過節總有很多美味的餸菜，如白切雞和豉油雞，但我最喜歡的是【滷水豬腳】。因為用文火長時間烹調後，滷水汁滲入豬腳裡，味道特別香濃；我最喜歡吃的就是惹味的小菜！我跟太太一樣，都是在恩平出生。雖然家裡是做藥材生意的，但我在十二歲左右便來了香港做裁縫學徒。要當學徒，先要給師父二百元白銀當學費。之後每天清晨五時便要起床，給師父準備熱水洗面，六時左右吃早飯，七時許，師父便開始工作。初時，師父沒有給我傳授任何技巧，我只負責做一些收拾和打掃的工作，於是只好在旁靜靜偷師。半年後，師父才正式教我縫製裁剪的技巧。學師期間是包伙食的，每天吃的都是比較清淡的蒸魚和青菜，偶然間會很想念家鄉的燒肉和雞。我用了整整三年時間才學滿師，但由於那時候正開始打仗，無奈之下只好回家鄉恩平去。回到恩平，我賣過故衣（即舊衫），每星期拿一大堆舊衣服到墟場（類似現時的大笪地）賣。也開過雜貨鋪，從恩平購入蔬菜果類等貨物，在廣州做買賣。我也開過中式茶樓。茶樓位於河邊，有些古惑的食客將吃完的蒸籠掉到河裡，於是結帳時便不用付錢。我當時只有十多歲，也沒他們法子。茶樓最後要結束，但並非生意失敗，而是遭「日本仔」（即日本軍人）路經時大肆破壞。茶樓沒有一樣東西是完整的，只有結束。戰爭終於結束，家裡的人整整齊齊地活著。我於是賣布為生，可惜最後蝕本而回。後來經朋友介紹到香港發展，當時我二十三歲，決定要做裁縫。兩年後和太太結婚，育有四名子女，太太負責日常家務，我負責養家。孩子大了會幫忙照顧弟妹，也會幫補學費。直到六十歲，我因為視力開始衰退，便退休了。但還清楚記得，我曾經為女兒縫製結婚晚禮服，也曾經為外孫女做花女的裙子！我跟兒女一樣愛吃，但我並不是從小便懂得煮食。來港後要自食其力，我又喜歡讀報，於是從報章的介紹中慢慢學會了烹調方法。從中學習、嘗試、改進，到最後總算有一點成績。【薑蔥焗魚腩】是家裡其中一道受歡迎的菜。雖然焗魚並不是什麼特別的家鄉菜，只是煮魚的一種新方法，但因為外層鬆化脆卜卜，內裡又保留到魚的鮮味和肉質，所以就連家裡的小孩子都很喜歡吃！

滷水是以多種香料煮成，用途廣泛的中式醬油。材料主要有花椒、八角、陳皮、桂皮、甘草、草果、沙薑、蒜、蔥、生抽、老抽及冰糖等，熬製數小時而成。一般相信滷水煮得越久越惹味，所以有的食店會每天加入新鮮材料與原來的滷汁同煮，反覆精煉成陳年滷汁。

I like preserved salted fish, shrimp eggs with pomelo skin and *fun guo* [a kind of steamed dumpling]. The filling is made with dried shrimps, peanuts, spring onions and diced pork. Once cooked, the dumplings can be kept for quite a while. That's why we always have them at home. They've become part of our daily meal. During festivals, we have

NEIGHBORHOOD

"Dark sauce" is made of pepper, anise, dried orange peel, cinnamon bark, licorice root, ginger, scallion and other ingredients. The longer the sauce is cooked, the better its taste.

many delicious dishes, like steamed chicken and soy sauce chicken. But Stewed Pig's Trotter in Dark Sauce is my favourite, because it has to be stewed for a long time, so the marinade penetrates deep into the pig's trotter and gives it a strong flavour. My wife and I were born in Enping in southern China. My family ran a Chinese herbal medicine shop. When I was twelve, I came to Hong Kong to be a tailor's apprentice. I paid the master two hundred dollars as a fee. I had to wake up at five in the morning every day to prepare hot water for my master to wash his face. At about six, we had breakfast, then at seven my master started working. At first, he wouldn't teach me anything. I simply cleaned up and kept the place tidy. I used to sit next to him and watch him work. After six months, he started teaching me sewing and tailoring. When I was an apprentice, I ate at the shop. We had plain food like vegetables and steamed fish. I missed the chicken and roast pork. I spent three years learning to become a tailor. About that time, the war began, so reluctantly I went back to Enping. I worked in the rag business. Every week, I would bring a lot of old clothes to the market to sell. I also ran a grocery shop. I bought fruit and vegetables in Enping and sold them in Guangzhou. I also had a tea house by the river. Sometimes, customers played tricks: after they'd finish their dim sum, they would throw the steam baskets the food was served in into the river so they wouldn't be counted in the bill. I was quite young and there was nothing I could do about it. The restaurant had to close in the end, not because business was bad, but because the Japanese destroyed most of it when they passed through. Afterwards, I tried to make money by selling cloth, but the business failed. Eventually, a friend convinced me to come back to Hong Kong. I was twenty-three years old and set up as a tailor. Two years later, I got married. We had four children. My wife took care of the household chores and I earned money for the family. As the children got older, they worked part-time to help out. I retired when I was about sixty. My eyesight was weakening. When my daughter got married, I made her an evening dress. I also made a floral dress for my granddaughter. My children and I love to eat. I didn't know how to cook when I was young. It was only after I came to Hong Kong that I began reading recipes in the newspapers—that's how I started learning to cook. I always tried to improve the recipes.

鹵水豬腳

豬腳1隻
滷水汁半支（200毫升）
清水400毫升
調味：糖、薑、酒適量

1 豬腳洗淨斬件，汆水
2 再走油，浸冷水，用手輕掃皮面，除去豬皮上的硬毛*
3 滷水汁加水煮滾後，下豬腳及調味料
4 慢火煮45分鐘，不時翻動豬腳，以防黏底，直至豬腳完全稔軟及上色**
5 收火，焗數分鐘

* 去除豬腳硬毛可用火燒刮，要小心不要燒傷指頭
** 滷水汁可置於冰箱內，循環再用2-3次。記著每次要先刮去表面的油層

Stewed Pig's Trotter in Dark Sauce

1 pig's trotter
200 ml Chinese marinade *(lo shui)*
400 ml water
some sugar, ginger and wine

1 Rinse pig's trotter, then cut into big pieces. Blanch, rinse and set aside.
2 Deep-fry pig's trotter until golden brown, then immerse in cold water. Lightly scrape surface to get rid of the thick, coarse hair*.
3 Boil marinade with water. Put in pig's trotter and remaining seasonings.
4 Simmer for 45 mins on low heat. Stir from time to time until the trotter is tender and has absorbed the Chinese marinade**.
5 Turn off heat and keep cover on for a few minutes.

** You can remove the coarse hair over a flame, but be careful not to burn your fingers.*
*** The Chinese marinade can be stored in the freezer and reused two to three times. Remember to skim off the top layer of oil each time before use.*

薑蔥焗魚腩

大鯇魚魚腩（重12兩，約480克）
蔥3兩（約120克）
薑2兩（約80克）
生粉2湯匙
紹興酒1茶匙
清水1/2杯
麻油少許
調味料：鹽、糖各1/2茶匙，生抽、老抽各1茶匙，胡椒粉少許

1 魚腩洗淨，瀝乾水，將一半的調味料及生粉與魚腩一齊撈勻
2 薑切片，蔥切段。落油燒熱鑊，放下薑片爆香撈起，將油繼續燒至冒煙，放下魚腩煎至金黃色，撈起瀝乾油*
3 將蔥段放入鑊內爆香，灑入酒，魚腩、薑片回鑊，落水，加入餘下的調味料，加蓋焗約10分鐘，用剩下的生粉加2湯匙清水勾芡，淋入麻油上碟

* 用薑蔥爆香，去魚腥味

Sauté Fish Head with Spring Onion and Ginger

480 g grass carp head
120 g spring onion, 80 g ginger
2 tbsps corn flour
1 tsp Shaoxing wine
½ cup water
½ tsp sesame oil
seasonings : ½ tsp each sugar and salt, 1 tsp each dark and light soy sauce, pinches pepper

1 Remove gills from fish and rinse. Chop fish head into two, then cut into long pieces. Marinade with half portion of seasonings and corn flour and mix well.
2 Slice ginger and section the spring onion. Pour oil into heated wok. Put in ginger slices and fry until fragrant; dish up. Heat oil until smoky, then put in the fish head pieces.
3 Put sectioned spring onion into wok and fry until fragrant; sprinkle in wine. Put in sautéed ginger slices and fish head*, add water and the remaining portion of seasonings. Cook for about 10 minutes with cover on.
4 Mix 2 tbsps of water with the remaining corn flour. Pour mixture in to form a gravy. Sprinkle with sesame oil, then serve.

** Sauté with ginger and spring onion to take away the "smell", thus making them fragrant, smooth and tender to taste.*

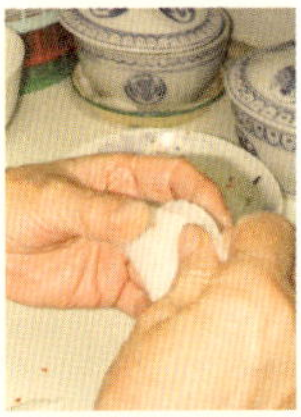

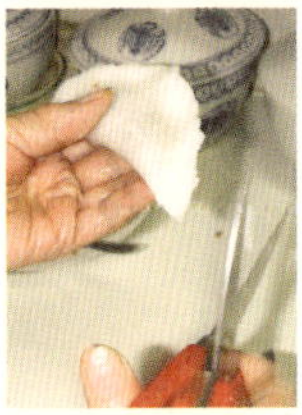

蒸粉果

雞肉*80克
紅蘿蔔及冬菇各40克
澄麵粉200克
大沸水3/4杯
鹽1/4茶匙
油少量
芫茜2棵
薑及蒜少量
調味：鹽1/2茶匙，酒、糖、粟粉、麻油適量

1 將雞肉、紅蘿蔔、芫茜、冬菇切碎粒**，以調味撈勻，用少量油、薑、蒜爆香成餡料，備用
2 將篩過的澄麵粉、鹽置大盤中，以沸水快速攪勻，放置案上5分鐘，之後加入少許油搓成軟滑粉糰***
3 將澄麵粉糰搓成長條，切為大小相同之小粒，以木棍輾薄成圓形，包入適量之餡料****
4 平碟塗上少量油，將包好之粉果放於碟上
5 大火蒸約3- 4分鐘，蒸好趁熱吃

* 不用雞肉，可素食
** 配料不可切得太大，否則會破皮
*** 小心熱粉糰燙手，可用保鮮紙隔著搓揉
**** 粉果餡忌油多、水多、粉多、芡大。油多皮邊難以黏合；水多餡身不乾結，製作困難；粉多失去肉類的鮮味；芡大則製成品會漏汁

Fun Guo (Steamed Dumplings)

80 g chicken*
40 g each carrots and winter mushrooms
200 g non-glutinous flour
¾ cup water
¼ tsp salt
some oil
2 stalks coriander
garlic and ginger to taste
seasoning : ½ tsp salt, wine, sugar, sesame oil and cornstarch to taste

1 Dice chicken, carrots, coriander and mushrooms**. Add seasonings and mix well. Heat a wok with a little oil and fry ginger and garlic until fragrant, then add the chicken mixture. Fry until cooked.
2 In a large bowl, combine sifted flour and salt. Pour in boiling water, stirring constantly. Let stand for five minutes, then add a little oil and knead*** into a soft dough.
3 Roll the dough into a long stick and cut into small pieces. Using a rolling pin, roll each piece into a circle and put some chicken mixture on top. Wrap into dumplings.****
4 Put dumplings on greased, flat plate.
5 Steam on high heat for three to four mins. Serve hot.

* *Chicken may be left out for vegetarians.*
** *The filling must be diced finely to avoid breaking the pastry.*
*** *Be careful of the hot dough. If necessary, use plastic wrap when kneading.*
**** *The filling shouldn't have too much oil, water, cornstarch or sauce. Otherwise, it may be difficult to seal the dumplings— the filling may be too moist, or the sauce may leak.*

唐新瑤　八十八歲　祖籍恩平

兒時吃的東西和一般廣東菜沒有很大的分別。並不是每天都大魚大肉，唯有大時大節如農曆新年和中秋，才可以吃到我愛的【南乳花生豬腳】。一大口肥而不膩的豬腳肉，是我最大的享受。雖然弄豬腳很費時，不過味道之佳，真的令我流口水。日常愛吃的還有豬油渣炒花生和辣椒菜脯，拌飯吃別有一番風味。豬油渣其實是把豬油膏煎乾而成，香脆可口，小朋友就最愛吃脆卜卜的東西。兒時不用「落手落腳」去耕田，十五六歲才有機會上學。二十歲的時候，日本軍到鄉下去捉「花姑娘」，專門找未婚的姑娘來作妓女。當時舅婆帶著我們女孩子逃到山頭那兒避難。兩年後經媒人介紹，認識了我的丈夫。1955年申請來港陪伴當裁縫的丈夫。做了家庭主婦，才認真學煮飯。【牛鰍魚木瓜湯】的材料很簡單，而且有益，可以潤肺，暖胃，對腸胃很好。常喝湯水身體健康，還滋陰養顏。這個湯沒有葛湯或苦瓜湯那種特別的味道，很易入口。我有四個兒女，卻不是每個都喜歡喝湯。兒女還小的時候，我要圍著檯追著他們，硬要他們喝湯。去探望婚後移居日本的大女兒時，我就準備了這個湯給她喝。

第二次世界大戰期間，或被迫或自願（或有償的）為日軍提供性服務的女性，是為「慰安婦」。慰安婦多來自中國大陸、台灣、滿洲國、韓國等地。不少慰安婦染上性病，有的由於多次墮胎，導致終生不孕。慰安婦還不時充當護士、腳夫以致被武裝起來充當炮灰。為掩蓋罪證，有些慰安婦被集體槍殺。

Tong Sun Yiu　88 years old　Hometown Enping

When I was young, our food was similar to Cantonese dishes. We often couldn't afford fish and meat, so we had to wait until festivals like Chinese New Year or Mid-Autumn to have my favourite dish: Stewed Pig's Trotter and Ground Nuts in Red Bean Curd. I used to eat big, big mouthfuls of pork fat. It gave me immense pleasure! Making pig's trotter takes a long time, but it tastes so good it's worth the wait. I also like to eat dregs of lard, fried peanuts, and chilli with preserved vegetables. They go well with rice. It is made from frying lard until it becomes dry. My children love it because it's crispy. When I was young, we didn't have to work in the fields, and when we were fifteen or sixteen, we could go to school. When I was twenty, the Japanese army came through looking for "flower ladies". They would grab single women to become prostitutes. My grand-aunt took all the girls to the mountains and hid us there. Two years later, I was introduced to my future husband through a match-maker. He was a tailor. In 1955, we came to Hong Kong. That's when I became a real housewife and learned how to cook. Flathead Fish and Papaya Soup has simple ingredients. It's nutritious and good for the lungs, stomach and digestive system. It helps keep you young. It has what I call a friendly taste. Not all of my four children like this soup. When they were small, I would chase some of them around the table, forcing them to have it. These days, when I visit my eldest daughter, who went to Japan after she got married, I make this soup for her.

During the Second World War, the Japanese army recruited or forced women to provide sex services. These women are known as "flower ladies" in Chinese and "comfort women" in English.

南乳花生豬腳

豬腳約3磅（1120克）
南乳2塊半
南乳汁2湯匙
薑幾片
蔥2棵（切段）
蒜3瓣（剁碎）
八角半個
米酒1湯匙
冰糖1小塊
鹽少許
粟粉適量
生抽 3 湯匙
清水 4 杯

1 蒜蓉放到南乳裡，加2勺水搗爛
2 鍋放油，炒香南乳汁
3 鍋裡放3杯水、米酒、薑、八角、冰糖、生抽、豬腳（參考「滷水豬腳」食譜的豬腳除硬毛方法）*
4 大火燒開轉小火，燜到豬腳稔軟（約2小時）
5 勾芡，讓汁煮濃
6 上碟，蔥放上面，澆上濃汁

* 這道菜一般和花生一起做，把泡了一小時的花生與豬腳一起放到鍋裡。如家中有人不能吃花生，可放泡好的黃豆或毛豆。

Stewed Pig's Trotter and Ground Nuts in Red Bean Curd

1½ kg pig's trotters
2½ pieces fermented red bean curd
few slices ginger
2 stalks spring onions, sectioned
3 cloves garlic, finely chopped
½ anise
1 tbsp rice wine
small piece rock sugar
1 tsp cornstarch
3 tbsps light soy sauce
4 cups water

1 Mix garlic and red bean curd with ½ cup of water. Mash.
2 Heat wok with oil, quickly fry red bean curd until fragrant.
3 Add 3 cups of water, rice wine, ginger, anise, rock sugar, light soy sauce, and pig's trotters.*
4 Bring to a boil, then set to low heat. Simmer for about two hours until pig's trotters turn soft.
5 Mix cornstarch with ½ cup of water. Add and cook until sauce thickens.
6 Mix well and serve. Garnish with spring onions, then drizzle with thickened sauce.

* *This dish goes well with peanuts. Soak the peanuts for about an hour and cook with the pig's trotters. If anyone is allergic to nuts, use soy beans instead.*

牛鰍魚木瓜湯

牛鰍魚 1 條（約450克）
煲湯木瓜 1 個（中）
果皮 1 小片
花生1/4杯
薑數片
油、鹽、胡椒適量
清水約10杯

1 先將魚洗淨，切成兩段，加鹽醃一會後用紙抹乾水
2 下油、薑片，慢火把魚煎至兩面金黃，加入清水 4 杯，大火燒至湯呈奶白色，熄火
3 把木瓜去皮，洗淨，切件
4 把魚和魚湯倒進容量4公升的湯鍋內，加入木瓜、花生、果皮、薑，加水過面(約8厘米)，大火燒開
5 撇去湯面上的浮沫，加蓋，改為小火，煮2小時至木瓜溶化
6 以鹽和少許胡椒粉來調味

其功效潤肺，暖胃，對腸胃好

Flathead Fish and Papaya Soup

1 flathead fish (450g)
1 papaya (medium size)
quarter size tangerine peel
some raw peanuts
few slices ginger
some pepper, salt and oil
10 cups water

1 Rinse fish, then cut in half. Sprinkle with salt. Leave for a few minues, then wipe dry and fry over medium heat.
2 Add oil and ginger slices. Fry fish on a low heat until golden yellow on both sides. Pour in four cups of water. Reset to high heat and keep boiling until water turns milk-white. Turn off heat.
3 Peel papaya, rinse and cut into big chunks. Throw aways the seeds.
4 Put the fish and soup in a four-litre stockpot. Add papaya, raw peanuts, tangerine peel and more ginger. Add more water until it's about 8cm above original water level. Bring to a boil.
5 Skim away surface froth. With cover on, reset to low heat and boil for about two hours until papaya gets soft and starts dissolving.
6 Add salt and pepper to taste.

This soup is good for digestion. It helps to warm the stomach and lungs.

到九廣鐵路工作，
最先負責清潔火車頭……

A friend helped me get a job at the Kowloon Canton Railway.
At first, I was responsible for cleaning the engines…

朱許紫　九十歲　祖籍增城

我在廣州鄉下讀完小學後，就離鄉找在香港工作的姐姐。當時我只有十多歲，幾經辛苦終於在一間辦館找到了一份幫工，起初什麼都不懂，又有很多工作要做，十分吃力。一個月後經人介紹到九廣鐵路工作，最先負責清潔火車頭，然後調職洗火車卡。幾年後日本侵略香港，姐姐到了新加坡，緊急情況下我便獨自返回家鄉。由於家鄉再沒有家人，所以暫住親戚家，後來由親戚介紹到中山做傳遞工作。太平後回到香港，朋友介紹下我到政府公務局機電工程處擔任計算工作。雖然工作表現良好，卻不幸受到裁員的影響。幸好得到一位同在公務局工作的外國人協助，才恢復原職。在這些艱辛的日子裡，住過不同的地方，有木屋、板間房、雙層床床位等等，最舒服是後來租到一個屬於自己的房子，不用再跟別人同住。不會在家煮食，通常是外出用膳，大部分時間都是到大牌檔。最喜歡各式碟頭飯。

以一個碟盛載餸菜及白飯，俗稱「碟頭飯」，通常附送餐湯或飲品，一般價錢，大眾口味，十分普遍，是港式快餐的代表。常見的款式有燒味飯、柱侯牛腩飯、咖哩雞飯、黑椒豬或牛排飯等。

Chu Hui Tsi　90 years old　Hometown Zengcheng

After I finished primary school in Guangzhou, I came to Hong Kong to live with my sister, who was working there. I eventually found a job as an assistant in a retail shop. I knew nothing at that time and there was a lot of work. It was very hard. After about a month, a friend helped me get a job at the Kowloon Canton Railway. At first, I was responsible for cleaning the engines, then I was assigned to cleaning the compartments. A few years later, the Japanese invaded Hong Kong. My sister went to Singapore. I had nowhere to go but back to my hometown, Zengcheng. I had relatives there, so I stayed with them and eventually got a job as a courier. After the war, I came back to Hong Kong. I got a job as a clerk with the Electronical and Mechanical Services Department. I did very well, but was laid off for a while. With the help of a Westerner who worked there, I eventually got my job back. I think back on those hard times, living in a wooden hut or a make-shift room, sharing a double-tiered bed with someone. The best time was when I rented a room of my own. I didn't have to share with anyone any more. I didn't cook at home in those days. I usually ate at *dai pai dongs*. These days, I like anything that goes with rice on a big plate.

Rice on a big plate is a colloquial term referring to a bed of rice with food on top. It is basically Cantonese fast food.

我年輕時曾幫手開餅鋪。

When I was young, I helped out at a bakery.

小時候，我常常吃切片蓮藕。好味道，又有鐵質，絕對是老人家的健康食品！年紀大了，咬不到蓮藕，就磨粉弄藕餅，也覺得非常好吃。以前我也會蒸給兒女吃，有的喜歡，有的卻說太淡了。有些孫兒愛吃濃味的，我會改用煎的方法，或跟臘腸一齊蒸。總之花盡心思，滿足他們的口味。其實，弄【蒸藕餅】一點都不難，沒什麼特別，一學就懂了！先將蓮藕磨成蓉，並預留兩薄片，蒸熟後作裝飾用；把雞肉剁碎，瑤柱蒸熟後再撕成幼絲，杞子洗淨備用。加入蓮藕蓉、雞蓉、鹽、糖及生粉各半茶匙作調味，並攪拌成膠狀。水滾後蒸約二十分鐘；蒸熟後，灑上瑤柱絲、杞子，即可食用。蒸藕餅加臘腸，味道較濃，煎的則香口惹味，悉隨尊便。我年輕時曾幫手開餅鋪，工作了二十多年。入行時，對做餅一點認識都沒有。當時我不喜歡餅鋪的傳統做角仔方法，所以自己想出一個鬼主意，引進西法用酥皮做角仔，就是用椰絲、砂糖、芝麻、豬油加麵粉搓製，然後烘焗。很多客人都喜歡，令我覺得非常開心。但是，我還是最喜歡吃蒸藕餅。

蓮藕是多年生草本植物荷花的地下莖，微甜而脆，可生食也可做菜，藥用價值相當高。蓮藕在中國文化中亦有特殊的意義，除以「藕斷絲連」形容關係之難解難分外，亦有不少詠荷的作品：「中通外直，不蔓不枝……出污泥而不染，濯清漣而不妖」，被視為君子花。

麥張瑞意 八十三歲 家鄉新會

When I was young, we often had sliced lotus root. It tastes good and is full of iron. It's definitely a healthy food, especially for elderly people. It's a bit too hard for me now, but I can steam it and make patties. It's still very tasty. I used to make them for my children. Sometimes, they thought the patties were too plain, so I would cook them with Chinese sausages

and think of other ways to spice them up. It's not difficult to make. When I was young, I started helping out at a bakery, and I ended up working there for twenty years. When I started, I knew nothing about making cakes and bread. I didn't like the traditional way they made croquettes, so I used the Western way of making pastry and created our own, using shredded coconut, sesame, pork grease and flour. Many customers liked them, which made me very happy. But I still prefer Steamed Lotus Root Patties.

Lotus root (*lian ou*) tastes slightly sweet and is crispy. Raw or cooked, it is nutritious Lotus has a unique place in Chinese culture. For instance, the idiom *ou duan si lian* describes people who are apart but who have each other in their hearts, connected like the silky fibres of the root.

蒸藕餅

蓮藕約300克
雞肉約190克
薑蓉、瑤柱及杞子適量
調味：鹽1/2茶匙、糖1/2茶匙、生粉

1 瑤柱蒸熟後撕成幼絲
2 杞子洗淨備用
3 蓮藕磨成蓉，雞肉剁碎，加入調味，一同攪拌成膠狀*
4 平鋪於碟中，水滾後蒸約20鐘
5 熟後，灑上瑤柱絲、杞子即可**

* 可考慮加入臘腸，使菜式味道較濃，或改用煎的方法，較香口惹味
** 可預留兩薄片蓮藕，蒸熟作裝飾用

鳴謝：簡梁以瑚女士提供菜式及烹調方法

Steamed Lotus Root Patties

300 g lotus root
190 g chicken fillet
some chopped ginger, dried scallops and wolfberries
½ tsp each salt and cornstarch

1 Steam the dried scallops until cooked, then shred.
2 Rinse wolfberries and set aside.
3 Scrape and rinse lotus root, then mash. Mince chicken fillet. Mix lotus root mash and minced chicken with salt and cornstarch. Stir well until sticky.*
4 Form patties and place evenly on a plate and steam over boiling water for about 20 minutes**.
5 When cooked, sprinkle with shredded dried scallop and wolfberries. Garnish with the cooked sliced lotus roots and serve. To make it into a crispy dish, fry until golden brown.

* *To give the dish a stronger flavour, add preserved Chinese sausage.*
** *Keep aside 2 thin slices of lotus root. Steam until cooked and use as a garnish.*

Many thanks to Ms Evelyna Liang for the recipe.

你們知道大豐成雞欄在哪裡嗎？

I used to catch chickens that had escaped
while being unloaded at the Dai Fung Sing shed.

梁耀　七十五歲　家鄉太平

年輕時一家人住在住家艇，就幫忙落貨，把新鮮運到的生果從船上送到油麻地果欄，除賺到薪水，有時還有額外收穫。在果欄的生果最新鮮的了，我常常把生果放進汗衫裡，放得滿滿的，挺著個大肚腩把生果帶回家，不新鮮的都不拿呢！你們知道大豐成雞欄在哪裡嗎？那時雞販上貨時，總會有一、兩隻走丟了，走到水溝裡去，我就把牠們捉起拿回住家艇，讓太太放在碳爐上蒸，那就是【金針雲耳蒸雞】。我二十歲不到便結婚，育有五女三子。現時退休了，與太太和小兒子住在秀茂坪，每天就到中心打發時間。一星期內我最愛星期四，因為星期四中心會廉價售賣義工弄的甜點。甜點正是我的心頭好呢！

果欄建於1913年，位於油麻地，為兩層高具戰前特色的石建築組群，曾是九龍水果批發市場。於1990年代中，批發市場搬往長沙灣副食品批發中心，但依然有不少批發商在油麻地果欄繼續經營。政府曾考慮清拆果欄，並與對面已停業的油麻地戲院及鄰近的露宿者之家（紅磚屋）一起發展，但由於果欄搬遷計劃仍存爭議，故先行發展油麻地戲院和紅磚屋地段。

Leung Yiu　75 years old　Hometown Taiping

When I was young, our family lived on a boat. I used to help unload fresh fruit from the boat at the wholesale market in Yau Ma Tei. I not only earned a salary, but sometimes a bonus of fruit. The fruit there was the freshest. I would use my T-shirt to carry it home. I got married before I was twenty. We have five daughters and three sons. Sometimes, I caught chickens that had escaped while being unloaded at the Dai Fung Sing shed. They would hide around the waterways. I'd catch them and take them back to our boat for my wife to steam on a charcoal stove. She would make Steamed Chicken with Dried Lily Flower and Black Fungus. Now I'm retired and live with my wife and our youngest son in Sau Mau Ping. I spend time at the social centre every day. I like Thursdays the best because they sell desserts made by volunteers at a low price. Desserts are my favourite.

金針雲耳蒸雞

雞半隻
金針及雲耳各半兩
薑2片
蔥2棵（切段）
調味：鹽1/2茶匙，生抽1茶匙半，
糖及生粉各1茶匙

1 金針去梗*，與雲耳洗淨浸軟
2 雞洗淨，吸乾水分
3 加入調味料，雞與金針、雲耳、薑片拌勻
4 隔水蒸熟後，撒上蔥段便可上桌

* 可將金針逐條打結後蒸，會更爽更好味

Steamed Chicken with Dried Lily Flower and Black Fungus

half chicken
20 g dried lily flowers
80 g black fungus
2 slices ginger
few stalks spring onions, sectioned
seasonings : ½ tsp salt, 1½ tsps light soy sauce, 1 tsp sugar, 1 tsp cornstarch

1 Remove head from dried lily flowers*. Wash and soak with black fungus until soft.
2 Wash and clean chicken. Cut into pieces and wipe dry.
3 Mix the seasonings well with dried lily flowers, black fungus and ginger slices.
4 Steam over boiling water until cooked. Sprinkle with sectioned spring onions and serve.

* *It will be crunchier and tastier if the dried lily flowers are tied in a knot.*

日後我到商行工作，這點點日文倒派上用場。

I studied the language for just five or six months, but it was good enough to use when I worked in a trading company.

小時候，我在香港接受教育，但只讀至小學四年級，便因打仗而被迫失學。我的學校嶺東小學是一所私校，現在已經不在了。自問讀書成績不錯，因為父親會教我讀書認字。父親識字多，他曾在商船當買辦，也在警署做過傳話，即是中英文傳譯，所以功課有不明白的地方，我都會問他。記得讀四書古文時，父親就坐在我的隔鄰，他一邊看報紙，一邊聽我讀書。當遇到不懂的字句，我會裝傻跳過不讀，可是往往逃不過父親的耳朵，只好在他的督促下重讀一遍。打仗期間，父親要我學日文。雖然只學了五、六個月，但日後我到商行工作，這點點日文倒派上用場。即使今天已把學過的日文忘掉了，但我仍然覺得日文比英文易學。年輕時，我和家人住在「灣仔大馬路」，即今天的皇后大道東附近。打仗期間在街上遇見日本軍人就要行禮，不可走避，否則會被他們捉著，被迫向他們敬禮。三年零八個月的日子好艱苦啊，如果戰事多延續一個月，恐怕我已死於饑荒。幸好當時有配給柴證、米證，我們可以憑證換些食物，日子總算撐得過去。當時每人可獲分配的米糧只有六兩四。糧食是用煉奶罐來作量杯的，一點一滴都非常珍貴。政局不穩日子，我會留在家幫忙。情況好一點的時候，我會跟家人排隊取米糧或奶粉。當時搶食物的情況很平常，有些人等人家付了錢買東西之後就來搶。可能買來的人還未把食物放到口邊就被搶了，而搶食物的人不會跑，因他們急著把食物吃進肚子裡。當時物資有限，我最愛吃牛奶餅乾。那時的牛奶其實是煉奶開水，餅乾則是普通不過的梳打餅。長大後，我開始學烹調，其中令我印象深刻的是【大豆芽菜炒豬肉鬆】，因為這是母親傳授的菜式，或許不怎麼特別，製作亦簡單，但始終也是我的最愛。

My school was called Ling Tung Primary School. It was a private school. It no longer exists. I was quite good at school because my father used to teach me to read. He knew many, many words. He was a merchandiser on a commercial vessel, and he had also been a translator at the police station. When I got stuck with

those ancient texts, I would ask him for help. He would sit beside me, reading the newspaper while I read aloud the ancient texts. I could never fool him! When I came to words that I didn't know, I tried to skip the entire paragraph. But he knew right away! I had to read it over again. During the war, he asked me to learn some Japanese. I studied the language for just five or six months, but it was good enough to use when I worked in a trading company. I have totally forgotten it, but I remember it was easier than English to learn. When I was young, my family lived on the Big Avenue in Wanchai. That means Queen's Road East. When we ran into Japanese soldiers on the streets, we had to salute them. Otherwise, they would summon us to return and salute them. Those were difficult days. If the war lasted one month longer, we probably would have starved to death. There used to be ration tickets for wood and rice. Every person was rationed to have about six taels [240 g]. We used an empty condensed milk can as a measuring cup. Each grain was very precious. We managed. During the political upheaval, I stayed at home to help with the work. When the situation stabilized, I would stand in line with my family to get the rice. Some people got robbed once they paid for the food. Sometimes food would be grabbed from you just before it reached your mouth. Those who robbed didn't run away with your food: they would quickly swallow it. I used to love milk biscuits. But the milk at that time was actually condensed milk with water. The biscuits were simple soda crackers. When I grew up, I started learning how to cook. I remember Sautéed Soya Bean Sprouts with Chopped Pork very well because my mother taught me that. It was an ordinary dish and simple to make.

A tael is a measurement (about 38g) and in the past, a monetary unit (1.3 ounces of standard silver).

大豆芽菜炒豬肉鬆

枚頭肉150克
大豆芽菜120克
蔥花2茶匙
薑蓉2茶匙
蒜蓉2茶匙
上湯1/2杯
鹽、味粉、紹興酒、胡椒粉、麻油、生粉及油適量

1 先將大豆芽菜切去根，然後切粒
2 再將肉切碎為米粒形，用生粉把肉粒拌勻
3 用油起鑊，將拌勻的肉粒放在鑊中炒透
4 加入紹興酒，注入上湯，用鹽和味粉調味，候熟，連汁鏟起
5 將芽菜粒放在鑊中烘乾（去其寒氣），然後放入薑蓉炒勻
6 再將煮熟的肉粒連汁一起倒入鑊中，加入蔥花，蓋上鍋蓋
7 待芽菜熟後，撒上胡椒粉，用生粉勾芡，加麻油，和勻後便可上碟

Sautéed Soya Bean Sprouts with Chopped Pork

150 g loin of pork
120 g soya bean sprouts
2 tsps spring onion, finely chopped
2 tsps each ginger and garlic both minced
½ cup clear broth
some salt Shaoxing wine, pepper, sesame oil, cornstarch and oil

1 Cut root from soya bean sprouts, chop finely.
2 Chop pork into size of rice grain and mix with cornstarch.
3 Heat wok with oil. Stir fry the diced meat thoroughly.
4 Sprinkle with Shaoxing wine, pour in clear broth, add salt and chicken powder to taste. When done, transfer to a dish.
5 Fry the finely chopped soya bean sprouts in a dry wok, then pour in the minced ginger, fry quickly.
6 Add to wok the diced pork with sauce together with the finely chopped spring onion. Cover.
7 When soya bean sprouts are cooked, sprinkle with pepper. Add cornstarch water with sesame oil. Mix and serve.

我在五金廠工作了數十年，
閒時愛與工友到荔枝角游夜水。

In the evenings,
we would sometimes go to Lai Chi Kok for a night swim.

鄧景　八十歲　祖籍南海

解放後我與兄弟來到香港，親戚介紹我當木工學徒。我當時與另一個學徒睡在鋪頭裡，早上起來出外買餸煮飯給師父吃，九點吃過飯後便開始工作，熬到五點收工再做晚飯。有時師父不滿意我們煮的東西，便丟兩毫子給我們去買腐乳回來拌飯吃，心裡挺不好受的。後來透過朋友的介紹，在一家大五金廠當學徒，一天三餐都在工廠裡與其他工友一起吃，再不用自己燒柴煮飯，學滿師後更可到外面用餐。最愛到附近茶樓吃點心，當時一碟叉燒飯不過三毫，白粥鬆糕只是豆零，餓的時候就吃盅飯。我在五金廠工作了數十年，閒時總愛與工友到荔枝角泳棚游夜水，還喜愛與工友打賭看誰可待在深水處最久呢！現時我已退休，但太太還要上班，我便在家中掌廚，做飯給年紀尚幼的兒女吃。幼子最愛認叻，幼稚園時竟跟我說要到同學家中教他怎樣使用電腦！小孩子揀飲擇食，也拿他沒有辦法，他最愛吃雞翼、牛丸、腸仔，每次總把我煮的食物吃精光，有次還要求我弄番茄薯仔湯，但不喜歡的餸菜卻碰都不碰一下呢。

泳棚一般以竹搭成，於海面上建有小橋方便泳客下水，部分更設有更衣室、儲物櫃。20世紀初在香港甚為流行。1911年香港中華遊樂會於北角七姊妹道海邊設置泳棚，每年吸引的泳客達10萬人次。至60年代，政府收回部分泳棚土地重新發展，在各區興建多座公眾泳池，加上海港污染漸趨嚴重，令泳棚逐漸式微。1988年，泳艫團體向香港政府申請，並獲批准在西環域多利道重開泳棚，為香港市區現存唯一的泳棚。

After the communists took over, I came to Hong Kong with my brother from China and, with the help of a relative, became an apprentice carpenter. I slept above the shop, along with another apprentice. Every morning we would go the market to buy groceries, then come back and cook for our master. At about nine o'clock, after we'd eaten, we'd start work. In the evening, we made dinner. If our master

was unhappy with what we'd cooked, he would give us twenty cents to buy fermented bean curd to go with the rest of the rice. That always made my heart sink. Later, a friend helped me get a job as an apprentice at a big hardware factory. I had three meals a day at the factory with my colleagues. Once we'd completed our apprenticeship, we could even eat out. I loved to have *dim sum* in nearby restaurants. A plate of roasted pork on rice was just thirty cents. A bowl of congee with Steamed Sponge Cake was just five cents. When I was hungry, I would have a pot of rice. I worked at the factory for several decades. In the evenings my colleagues and I would sometimes go to Lai Chi Kok for a night swim. We would bet on who could stay in the deep water for the longest! I'm retired now, but because my wife still works, I take care of the cooking at home for our young children. My young son is very choosy about his food, but he loves chicken wings, beef balls and sausages. Sometimes, I make him potato and tomato soup, but he won't touch anything he doesn't like.

蒸鬆糕

麵粉320克
發粉3茶匙
糯米粉6湯匙
黃砂糖240克
清水1杯半

1 把糖和水煮溶，冷卻備用
2 將麵粉，發粉及糯米粉篩勻，加入已冷卻的糖水攪勻成糊狀
3 在小碗或錫紙杯內抹上油，把粉糊分放在內至滿
4 置於蒸籠內用大火蒸15分鐘，冷卻後倒出即成

Steamed Sponge Cake

320 g flour
3 tsps baking powder
6 tbsps glutinous flour
240 g granulated brown sugar
1½ cups water

1. Heat sugar in water until it dissolves. Let cool and set aside.
2. Mix flour, baking powder and glutinous flour. Sift, then add the cooled sugar mixture. Mix well to form a paste.
3. Spread oil in small bowls or tin-foil cups. Put paste in each cup until full.
4. Steam for 15 minutes on high heat. Let cool, take out and serve.

我八歲開始就到市集買菜，
回家煮飯給家人吃。

When I turned eight,
I began working at home and cooking for my family.

駱群卿　八十三歲　祖籍東莞

八十多年來，我從未打過一份工，八歲開始就擔起持家的重責。母親和大姐要到地盤運泥沙，父親每天就給我錢到市集買菜，回家煮飯給家人吃。幸有好鄰里，一直關照著我們。那時多買魚骨回家煲湯，因為比較便宜。那是我最喜歡的【魚骨枸杞湯】。到現在，那仍是我最珍愛的食物之一。十二歲，跟著哥哥到香港，幫手看家和做家務。阿嫂因要出外工作，一頭家的勞務又落到小小年紀的我身上。幸好兩年後，哥哥讓我上學，讀了兩年半書，總算識字，能書能寫。二十歲左右，在家人安排下結婚，一直照顧孩子做家務。現在兒女都已長大，有自己的家庭。以前還會吃淡水魚，現在卻喜歡海水魚，覺得更鮮味。兒子最愛吃我親手剁的【冬菜牛肉餅】，常常要求我做給他們吃。講到食，最記得小時候吃過炒米餅、鬆糕和雞屎藤茶果等。那時很少機會吃，所以曾趁母親看不到時偷來吃。始終傳統糕點最美味，也許懷念的，還有那能夠「調皮」玩耍的日子吧！

When I turned eight, I began working at home and cooking for my family. My mother and eldest sister worked at a construction site, carrying mud. My father gave me money every day to buy food from the market. I usually bought fish bones to make soup. They were cheap. My favourite was Soup with Fish Bones and Matrimony Vine (*kau kei*). It's still

my favourite now. I came to Hong Kong with my brother when I was twelve and looked after his family, doing household chores, because my sister-in-law had to work. Two years later, my brother let me go to school. I studied for two-and-a-half years and learned to read and write. When I turned twenty, my family arranged for me to get married. I stayed home, bringing up the children and taking care of the housework. Our children are all grown up now and have their own families. I used to like fresh-water fish, but now I prefer sea fish. My son loves Steamed Minced Beef Cake with Spiced Cabbage. He always asks me to make it. I still remember the rice cookies, steamed sponge cakes and Fevervine Herb Cha Guo, snakes my mother would make for us when I was young. I used to steal a piece or two when she wasn't looking. Traditional *dim sum* is the best. I miss those days when I simply played and fooled around!

Fevervine herbs grow in moderate and humid areas, like Hong Kong.

魚骨枸杞湯

枸杞菜450克（12兩）
杞子少許
魚骨1-2條（中型）
清水4杯
薑、蒜、油、鹽、豆粉適量

1 洗淨枸杞菜，瀝乾水分備用
2 洗淨魚骨，用油、鹽、豆粉抹勻
3 用薑、蒜起鑊，煎香魚骨
4 另一鍋中注入清水4杯、薑2片，以大火滾起
5 水滾後下魚骨
6 水再滾後轉中火，下枸杞菜
7 杞子灼熟，下鹽調味即可

Soup with Fish Bones and Matrimony Vine

450 g matrimony vine
a few wolf berries
40-80 g fish bones
4 cups water
4 slices ginger
2 cloves garlic
1 tsp each oil, salt and cornstarch

1 Rinse the vine, blend well in a blender, strain and set aside.
2 Rinse fish bones. Mix with oil, salt and cornstarch.
3 Fry 2 slices of ginger and the garlic in a heated wok with oil. Fry fish bones until fragrant.
4 Pour 4 cups of water into a pot. Add 2 slices of ginger and bring to the boil.
5 Put fish bones in boiling water.
6 When water boils, set to medium heat and put in matrimony vine.
7 Parboil wolfberries and add salt to taste.

冬菜牛肉餅

免治牛肉284克（約10安士）
馬蹄3-4個
冬菜一小撮
調味：鹽、糖各1/2茶匙，蛋白1湯匙，清水2湯匙，粟粉、麻油及胡椒粉少許

1 馬蹄去皮切碎粒，備用
2 冬菜略為清洗，稍去鹹味
3 免治牛肉*加入調味、清水、粟粉、馬蹄粒及冬菜拌勻
4 盛碟中，弄平，大火隔水蒸約5至6分鐘便成

* 可加入少許免治豬肉來增加口感，但要略為增加蒸煮時間

Steamed Minced Beef Cake with Spiced Cabbage

284 g minced beef*
few water chestnuts
spoonful of spiced cabbage
seasonings : ½ tsp each salt and sugar, 1 tbsp egg white, some cornstarch, sesame oil and pepper, 2 tbsps water

1 Peel water chestnuts and dice. Set aside.
2 Rinse spiced cabbage.
3 Add seasonings to minced beef. Mix well with spiced cabbage and diced water chestnuts.
4 Place mixture on a plate and flatten. Steam over boiling water for 5-6 minutes, then serve.

** Substituting beef with minced pork will enhance the texture, but takes a little longer to cook.*

一早起來與一班伙記坐車到元朗飲早茶，
回來後就開始鬼佬茶市。

Usually, we woke up early in the morning and went to Yuen Long for morning tea.

韓國旋　八十一歲　祖籍番禺

隨兄長來港生活後，我便於親戚位於赤柱的食店當樓面。顧客來到海鮮餐館，總愛吃【一魚三味】，紅燒魚頭，上乾生粉炸，十分香脆可口；魚肉弄成斑球以菜或勝瓜炒，魚骨與豆腐仙菇煮湯。通常用兩至三斤的石斑，或用龍躉來做一魚三味，魚夠大才有肉弄斑球呀！煲粥當然用泥鯭，做湯底則用沙灌魚，熬出來白白的，很好看，小蝦頭則用來炒飯，燒賣上的蝦也是小蝦頭呢！後來朋友介紹我到太白海鮮舫工作。在那裡工作舒服又開心。一早起來與一班伙記坐車到元朗飲早茶，回來後就開始鬼佬茶市。當時外國旅行團是一車車的來到海鮮舫，旅客總喜愛上船坐一坐，飲飲啤酒。海鮮舫每天都有不少外國遊客來訪，我愛與他們攀談兩句，從中學到不少外語：鯛魚是Snapper，蔬菜是vegetables，還有Arigatou（日語）呢！晚上睡覺時陣陣海風，風涼水冷，多舒服！打風時就糟了，記得91年打風，連做廚房的那艘艇也被吹走，伙記都要上岸暫避。現時我已退休，但在艇上工作真是有趣！

太白海鮮舫及珍寶海鮮舫是香港仔深灣兩艘著名的海上畫舫，香港南區名勝。「海鮮舫」前身是「歌堂躉」。20年代起，水上人開設酒樓，受商賈歡迎，生意滔滔。50年代全盛時期，就有十多艘海鮮舫停泊在香港仔避風塘，規模最大就是珍寶和太白海鮮舫。珍寶海鮮舫亦有「世界最大海上食府」之稱，曾吸引不少中外名人光顧，如英女皇伊利沙伯二世、湯告魯斯等。1971年，珍寶海鮮舫發生大火，整艘焚毀，導致32人死亡，13人失蹤，及後重修。

I came to Hong Kong with my older brother. I worked as a waiter at a seafood restaurant owned by one of our relatives in Stanley. One of its specialities was One Fish, Three Styles. The fish head is braised, then coated with flour and deep-fried so it's crispy and spicy. The flesh of the fish is made into balls and fried with vegetables or squash. Finally,

the fish bones are made into soup with tofu and mushrooms. The best sort of fish to use is a garoupa of two to three catties of *lung den* fish. It has to have enough flesh to make the fish balls. *Nai mang* fish is best for the congee, and *sha koon* fish is good for the soup. The soup is white and looks very nice. Later, a friend helped me get a job at the Tai Pak floating seafood restaurant in Castle Peak Bay. It was good working there. We lived on board. Usually, we woke up early in the morning and went to Yuen Long for morning tea. Then we'd go back to the restaurant and get ready for the *gwei lo* [white-skinned westerners] *yum cha* [having *dim sum*] session. These tourists came in busloads, one after another to have *dim sum*. I liked talking to them and I learned quite a few foreign words. At night, when we went to bed, there was usually a nice cool sea breeze. How pleasant! Of course, it was terrible when the typhoons came. In 1991, we all had to take shelter on land.

一魚兩味

石斑魚1條（約600克）
紅蘿蔔數片
菜薳10棵
蒜蓉2茶匙
炸豆腐8－10件
小棠菜5－6棵
薑數片
韭黃、蔥段適量
醃料：鹽1/2茶匙，花雕酒、薑汁各1茶匙，胡椒粉、生粉、麻油適量
調味：生抽2茶匙、蠔油1湯匙、糖1茶匙、麻油適量、水半杯

預備

1 石斑魚洗淨，抹乾水，切出魚腩留用，做紅燒魚腩
2 起出魚肉，切大塊，備用炒斑球

炒斑球做法

1 放入鹽（1/4茶匙）、花雕酒及薑汁（各1茶匙）、胡椒粉少許，醃石斑塊15分鐘
2 菜薳用油鹽水灼熟，瀝乾水分，伴碟用
3 燒熱油爆香蒜蓉2茶匙，放入石斑塊、紅蘿蔔炒熟上碟

紅燒魚腩做法

1 魚腩加入鹽（1/4茶匙）、麻油及胡椒粉少許，醃20分鐘；然後沾生粉，用油炸至金黃色，備用
2 小棠菜用油鹽水灼熟，瀝乾水分，伴碟用
3 燒熱油爆香薑片、蔥段，下酒，加入調味煮滾，加入魚腩煮熟，下韭黃，便可食用

One Fish, Two Styles

600 g garoupa
several slices carrots
10 stalks *choi sum*
2 tsps minced garlic
8 - 10 pieces fried tofu
5 - 6 stalks *siu tong choi*
several slices ginger
some chives, shredded spring onions
marinade : ½ tsp salt, 1 tsp each Shaoxing wine and ginger extract, some white pepper, cornstarch and sesame oil
seasonings : 2 tsps light soy sauce, 1 tbsp oyster sauce, 1 tsp sugar, some sesame oil, ½ cup water

Preparation

1 Clean and dry garoupa. Separate the belly for Braised Fish Belly.
2 Fillet the rest of the fish into large slices for Fried Garoupa.

Fried Garoupa Directions

1 Season garoupa fillet for 15 minutes with ¼ tsp of salt, 1 tsp each of Shaoxing wine and ginger extract and a pinch of white pepper.
2 Cook *choi sum* in oil and salt water. Drain, then dry and set aside as garnish.
3 Heat oil in wok and fry minced garlic until fragrant, then add garoupa fillet and carrot slices. Pan-fry until cooked. Serve with cooked vegetables on the side.

Braised Fish Belly Directions

1 Season fish belly for 20 minutes with ¼ tsp of salt, sesame oil and pinch of white pepper. Coat lightly with cornstarch, then fry until golden. Set aside.
2 Cook *siu tong choi* in oil and salt water. Dry and use as garnish.
3 Heat oil in wok and fry ginger slices and shredded spring onions until fragrant. Sprinkle in wine and add the seasonings. Bring to a boil, then add fish belly and fried tofu and braise until cooked. Add chives and serve with *siu tong choi* on the side.

要善待伙計，善待他人。

I still remember my mother saying
how important it is to treat your employees well.

盧簡慧敏　八十七歲　祖籍山東

我最喜歡吃的是媽媽弄的【紅燒獅子頭】，簡簡單單的一斤肉三小球，以燴上海小棠菜伴碟，再加上一點色彩：漂亮的紅椒絲、青椒絲，紅紅綠綠的令人胃口大開。每次吃都記起伙頭弄給我們吃，又想起媽媽煮，自己又喜歡吃，於是便在腦中記下來了。我生於上海，爸爸過世後一家便靠在英租界開辦館維持，當然還得一班老伙計的照顧。一直記住母親的話：要善待伙計，善待他人。現在看過老人中心有什麼節目轉頭便忘掉，參加元朗旅行抽籤也要其他人提醒，但媽媽的話到現在還句句在心中。二次大戰戰火蔓延，澤北唐界起火時，九歲的我便在新年與家人由英租界走難到法租界。當年在廣州的姐姐寄了許多臘味回老家，走難時家中的叔叔說：「嘩！今年大小姐寄這麼多臘味回來，怎知要走了，沒有口福。」輾轉一家五口乘貨船到廣州投靠大姐，船錯誤地駛進黑龍江，波濤洶湧的江水把船搖晃得像一隻紙船，年幼的弟弟就這樣子嚇壞了，連醫生也幫不到。在廣州一住數年，習慣了「東方小巴黎」十里洋場的西化優雅生活，又怎能適應廣州的傳統樸實？兩地什麼都不同，完全不同，住的不同，地方不同。大家姐為了我們要多次搬屋，人多便要搬，一年搬兩次，我細細個都覺得煩，所以在廣州一住便是多年。和平後一家平安回到上海，過沒多久，共產黨於1949年建立中華人民共和國，我二十多歲就到香港投靠姐姐，在家與工人幫忙看顧十三個姨甥。後來結了婚，至今五十多年了，丈夫在李嘉誠寫字樓工作，人隨和得很，吃方面從不挑剔。我們如何認識？結婚幾十年了，誰記得這麼多呢！

清末民初中國積弱，曾與其他國家簽訂了一系列的條約，把國內部分土地出租給他國，設立租界，通常是沿岸地區，讓外國通商貿易。早自1840年鴉片戰爭，中國與英國簽訂《南京條約》開始，租界內可讓租借國自治管理，區域內的外國居民能行使獨立完善的行政及司法權。有時租界亦成為一些持不同政見者的避難所。

I love to sing and travel. And I love Stewed Minced Pork Balls in Brown Sauce [commonly known as Lion's Heads]. It's a simple dish made from pork divided into balls. Shanghainese *pak choi* adds colour. You also use shredded red chilli and green pepper. It's mouth-watering. I remember our cook making it for us when we were young. I also remember my

mother making it. I like it a lot—that's why I remember how to make it. I was born in Shanghai. After my father died, we opened a shop in the British Settlement area with the help of some of my father's old employees. My memory isn't always good these days, but I still remember my mother saying how important it is to treat your employees and others with kindness. During the Second World War, when I was about nine, the battle front drew closer and closer to us. There was a big fire in the Chinese Territory. During New Year, my family escaped into the French Settlement. My sister was living in Guangzhou at the time and she used to send us lots of preserved meat. When we fled, my uncle said, "Big sister sent so much food home, but our mouths are not blessed because we have to leave." Not long after, the five of us took a cargo ship to Guangzhou to stay with my sister. At one stage, the ship mistakenly sailed into Heilongjiang, in Northeasten China. The waves tossed the ship like a paper boat. My younger brother went all pale! We stayed with my sister in Guangzhou for a few years, but having been accustomed to the elegant Western life in Shanghai, known as the "Little Paris of the Orient", there was no way we could fit in with the simple, traditional life in Guangzhou. Everything was different—where we lived, the places. We ended up staying in Guangzhou for several years, although we moved a few times because there were so many of us. After the war, we went back to Shanghai. But then the communists came to power. That was 1949. When I was a little over twenty, I came to Hong Kong to live with another sister. I stayed at home and helped the maid take care of my thirteen nieces and nephews. Eventually, I got married. That was more than fifty years ago now. My husband worked in one of Li Ka Shing's businesses. My husband is very nice and is never choosy about what he eats. The funny thing is that I can't even remember how we met.

In the 19th century, the Qing Dynasty, China was forced into several treaties with European countries. These mandated the lease of a number of territories, predominantly coastal cities. After the Opium War (1840), for instance, China and Britain signed the Treaty of Nanjing, which marked the cession of Hong Kong to Britain as a crown colony.

Stewed Minced Pork Balls in Brown Sauce

600 g meat from leg of pork (70% lean; 30% fat)
a few pieces dried scallops
2-3 stalks Shanghai *pak choi*
1 egg white
some red and green chilli peppers (sliced thin)
4 cups oil
2 tsps water chestnut flour
some sugar, Shaoxing wine, cornstarch and light and dark soy sauce
1 tbsp water

1. Chop the pork roughly into small pieces.
2. Soak dried scallops until soft, then tear into shreds. Mix scallops and minced pork.
3. Add sugar, Shaoxing wine, cornstarch and light and dark soy sauce. Stir well. Add egg white to give the meat a smooth texture.
4. Shape pork into four to six balls.
5. Heat half the wok oil, then deep-fry pork balls briefly until golden brown and firm. Put in a casserole dish.
6. Add water until pork balls are half soaked. Add more dark soya sauce and Shaoxing wine. Simmer on low heat until tender and spongy*.
7. Mix water chestnut flour and water.
8. Trim and rinse Shanghai *pak choi* and parboil (with oil and hot water) with red and green chilli peppers.
9. Arrange the *pak choi* and peppers around the pork balls on a plate.
10. Stir the flour mixture on low heat to thicken. Pour over the pork balls and serve.

For best results, use a clay pot.

小巴黎紅燒獅子頭

上肉（7成瘦3成肥）1斤（600克）
瑤柱幾粒
上海小棠菜2-3棵
蛋1隻（只要蛋白）
紅椒青椒少許（切絲）
油4杯
馬蹄粉2茶匙
白糖、紹興酒、豆粉、生抽、老抽適量
清水少許

1. 將半肥瘦上肉剁碎（可用攪拌機）*
2. 瑤柱浸軟，拌入肉碎攪勻
3. 加入白糖、紹興酒、豆粉、生抽等調味拌勻，最好用老抽吊味，加入少許雞蛋白讓獅子頭滑一些
4. 把肉分成4至6個球（分成6個小球較容易做）
5. 用滾油泡一泡肉球，至表面呈金黃色，小球便不會散，亦更香口
6. 在砂鍋加入水，放入肉球，浸著球的一半，加入少許老抽、紹興酒，細火燜
7. 單是煮滾汁是不會好吃的，要把肉球燜到鬆和軟身才好吃
8. 上碟前，勾一個用馬蹄粉做的芡
9. 煮沸水，加少許油灼熟上海小棠菜和紅椒絲青椒絲，用來伴碟

* 獅子頭要鬆軟好吃，肉最好自己剁。七分瘦肉，三分肥肉，細切粗斬，大小如米粒，不能剁得太細，讓肉質間保持縫隙，才能含汁。另一個重點是容器，要細火燜，以砂鍋為最佳。

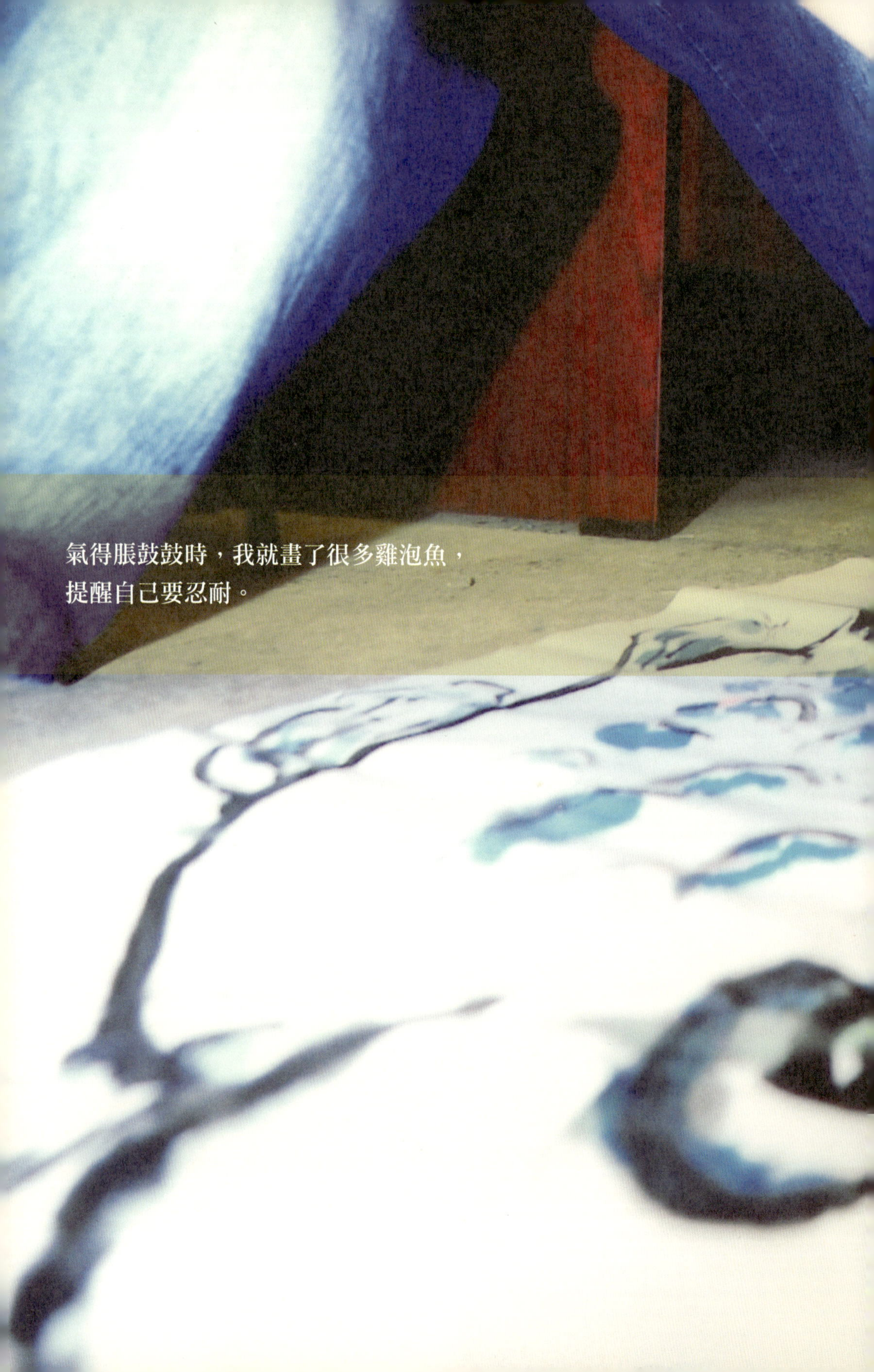

氣得脹鼓鼓時，我就畫了很多雞泡魚，
提醒自己要忍耐。

When I got angry, I would draw blowfish.
I used them to remind myself to be patient.

我又名「魚王」。小時候很喜歡繪畫，本來喜歡畫老虎，但是媽媽不喜歡，說「苦苦」聲，不好意頭。九歲那年，在美術課畫魚，老師給了100分，便開始畫魚，一畫就畫了幾十年。70年我曾在港台美術部和教育電視工作，那時候導演當我是機器，工作量很大，很受氣。氣得脹鼓鼓時，我就畫了很多雞泡魚，來提醒自己要忍耐。在眾多的魚類中，我最喜歡畫鯉魚，年年大「利」，年年有「餘」嘛。多年來，我最感謝的就是我老婆和一班老朋友的支持。最開心就是老婆常常陪我流連藝術場地。最記得有一次舉辦畫大魚行動，我朋友買了一塊60x40尺的布來支持我畫鯉魚。那一幅大畫曾在新世界中心足足展覽了三天。我自小家窮，跟父母寄居在姑婆家。姑婆是老師，頗為富有，但是非常刻薄。然而生活不全是悲慘，也有不少難忘的愉快故事。媽媽偶爾會到香港公幹，回來會買些餅乾給我吃。幾塊今天看似很普通的餅乾，我也覺得很好吃。提到食物，小時候我最喜歡就是媽媽做的木棉花糖水，甚至連那些乾木棉花也全吃個光。記憶中那些乾木棉花是很甜很甜的。每一次，媽媽總會說我頑皮，把沒有人吃的乾木棉花都放進我口裡。結婚後，我最喜歡吃老婆做的菜，尤其是【魚肉柚皮】，用鯪魚肉、果皮煎水煮成。街外的菜，根本不能和她做的相提並論。除了畫魚、吃魚，我也很喜歡釣魚。常常與老婆到南丫島旅行，租艇仔出海釣魚。吃自己釣的魚是最過癮、最美味的。每次去旅行的樂趣不單只在釣魚，因為老婆一定會帶著冰箱隨行，裡面放著她親手做的【椰汁馬豆糕】。我平日滴甜不沾，只有老婆弄的馬豆糕例外，椰汁新鮮，花奶又香，不軟不硬，很有口感。極品。

陳法興 七十一歲 祖籍西樵

初期香港離島仍未城市化，尚有翠綠山水，為假日避人的好去處。沿岸釣魚十分普遍，那時海域未嚴重污染，大部分漁獲皆可進食。

I'm also known as "Fish King". When I was young, I loved drawing. I liked to draw tigers, but my mother didn't like the sound of the word because she said it was inauspicious. [In Cantonese, "tiger" sounds like "bitter".] When I was nine, I drew a fish in art class and the teacher gave me the full one hundred marks. So, I kept drawing fish and I've been doing it

ITALY

for fifty-six years now. My family was poor, so my parents and I moved in with a grand-aunt. She was a teacher and was quite rich, but she was very mean. Life wasn't too bad though. We had some unforgettable and happy times. My mother sometimes worked in Hong Kong and would bring us back biscuits. A few ordinary biscuits tasted great to me. When I was young, I loved a sweet soup my mother made from the flowers of the cotton tree. I would even eat the dry flowers—my mother said I was very naughty, even though no one else wanted them. They were very, very sweet. After I got married, I loved eating what my wife cooked, especially Stuffed Pomelo Skin with Fish. No one can match the way she makes it. In the 1970s, I worked in the art department at Radio Television Hong Kong and Educational Television. The workload was heavy and I was often frustrated. When I got angry, I would draw blowfish. I used them to remind myself to be patient. I also love to draw carp [*lei* in Cantonese]. *Lei* sounds like "profit" and fish sounds like "abundance". So, my years are full of an abundance of profit. Over the years, I've had great support of my wife and many old friends. Apart from drawing and eating fish, I like fishing. My wife and I go to Lamma Island, where we rent a small boat. It's so enjoyable to eat what you catch yourself—it's always the most delicious. These trips are fun not only because of the fishing. My wife always brings along an ice box of Coconut Lentil Pudding that she makes. I seldom eat sweet things, but this is an exception. The coconut milk is fresh and the condensed milk smells good. The texture of the pudding is just right. It's a delicacy from heaven!

椰汁馬豆糕

馬豆60克
粟粉60克
糖120克
淡奶75毫升
椰奶250毫升
水275毫升

1 馬豆沖水，放沸水中，煲大約30分鐘至軟而不爛
2 將淡奶、椰奶及水拌勻
3 用少許以上汁液混合粟粉及糖
4 將其餘汁液加熱
5 把暖汁倒入混合的粉糊中，拌勻
6 粉糊倒回鍋中，用中火煮至糊面起泡，期間不停攪動
7 加入馬豆拌勻，盛在已浸過冷開水的糕盤內*
8 待完全冷卻後放進冰箱。馬豆糕凝固後，倒放在碟上切件吃

* 可改用小啫喱杯之類的容器，冷固後倒放，更受小孩子喜愛

Coconut Lentil Pudding

60 g split lentils
60 g corn flour
120 g granulated sugar
75 g fresh milk
250 g coconut milk
275 g water

1 Wash lentils. Cook in boiling water for about 30 minutes until soft but not mashed.
2 Mix fresh milk, coconut milk and water.
3 Mix corn flour and sugar with a little mixture from (2).
4 Heat remaining mixture from (2). Mix and stir.
5 Pour warm mixture from (4) into (3). Mix to form batter.
6 Transfer batter to pot. Cook on a medium heat until it bubbles. Keep stirring slowly during cooking.
7 Add in lentils. Pour mixture into a moistened (with cold cooked water) cake tray of your choosing.*
8 Let cool completely and chill in refrigerator. When set, turn upside down from cake tray on to a plate. Cut and serve.

* *Kids love them in small jelly cups!*

魚肉柚皮

柚皮1個
鯪魚肉70克
蛋1隻（打開拂勻）
薑1-2片
紅蘿蔔數片
芡汁：生抽、蠔油各1/2湯匙，糖1茶匙，雞湯1杯，生粉、麻油適量

1. 鯪魚肉加入少許糖、鹽、胡椒粉、麻油，拌勻，攪至起膠，備用
2. 柚皮切去青色外皮，放在一大鍋水內，大火煮沸，熄火，焗5-10分鐘，連水倒進另一鍋中，待冷
3. 用手在水中反覆壓出柚皮的水分，以便除去苦澀味；每壓一次，便換水一次。壓至水清及沒有苦澀味為止，約需換水十多次
4. 放柚皮在鑊中，柚外皮的那面需向下貼著鑊的表面，開火烘乾柚皮，然後切成長形塊狀
5. 在塊狀的柚皮中間切一刀，不要切斷，成雙飛狀的柚皮夾
6. 在柚皮夾內抹上蛋液，並釀入適量的魚肉*
7. 慢火煎柚皮魚肉夾，煎好後排放碟上，大火隔水蒸15分鐘
8. 用少許油，爆香薑及紅蘿蔔，加入芡汁煮滾後，淋在柚皮魚肉上，便可食用

* 可按個人喜好，在魚肉內加入蔥粒、蝦米粒或薑粒等材料

Stuffed Pomelo Skin with Fish

1 pomelo skin
70 g minced fish/dace flesh
1 beaten egg
1-2 slices of ginger
a few slices of carrot
seasoning : ½ tbsp each light soy sauce and oyster sauce, 1 tsp sugar, 1 cup chicken stock, sesame oil to taste and cornstarch to thicken sauce

1. Prepare fish paste.
2. Remove the green rind from the pomelo skin. Put the skin in a large pot of boiling water. Bring to a boil and turn off heat. Leave in pot with lid for about 10 minutes, then pour the water and skin into another pot to cool.
3. Press the skin inside the pot of water to remove the bitterness. Change the water after each pressing. Repeat until the water is clear and the skin is no longer bitter. It takes about 15 changes of water.
4. Put the skin in a wok, with the outer skin face down. Heat just enough to dry the skin, then cut into oblong pieces.
5. Score each slice without cutting through and fold into halves to create a sandwich effect.
6. Wet the inside of each piece with the beaten egg, then stuff with minced dace.*
7. Slowly pan-fry the stuffed pomelo pieces. Put them on a plate and steam on high heat for 15 minutes.
8. Heat wok with a little oil. Fry the ginger and carrot slices, then add the sauce. Bring to a boil and pour over the stuffed pomelo skin. Serve immediately.

** According to taste, add chopped spring onion, finely diced dried shrimp or chopped ginger to the minced dace.*

回味
I TASTE

冬天時，每天要四更起床燒柴煮飯，
五更把丈夫叫醒吃「五更飯 」。

I had to get up at four in the morning,
even during winter,
to prepare the fire to cook for him.

李潤 八十三歲 祖籍佛山疊滘

不要學煮飯，太辛苦啦！幸福的女性應當不用入廚。說起我少年時的入廚經驗，可又要哭一場呢。十多歲時，別的女孩仍是跑跑跳跳玩耍的日子，我就被揹入夫家作妾侍。丈夫從不踏足我房間，對他來說我好像只是家中的一位工人。有時，工人比我還好！冬天時，每天要四更起床燒柴煮飯，五更把丈夫叫醒吃【五更飯】。五更飯非常補身。之後我還要預備早飯，有時太累就坐在廚房睡著了。買菜、煮飯、熬湯、做點心，六十多年就如此度過。親朋戚友常笑說我做的菜比專業師傅的還要好，又說我做的粉果是全城最爽的，【黑芝麻糕】更是他們要求我做完又做的傳統糕點。我為家人預備的粥和湯水會隨著季節時令而有不同，但是他們總不吃那些湯渣。不知是否因為常常吃湯渣，現在我的身體仍很好，只有些微風濕。我天天還在廚房鑽來鑽去，都是煮給心愛的兒媳及親友吃。丈夫已九十多歲，需要輪椅出入，但對我也關愛多了。

古時為防盜賊，深夜會有人巡邏。分五個更次，每隔一更（兩小時）就會敲鑼報時。五更，就是清晨三至五時。

Cooking is such hard work. A woman who has someone to love her shouldn't have to slave away in the kitchen! I got married when I was ten. My husband, who already had one wife, kept me at home. He didn't even regard me as a maid in those days. I had to get up at four in the morning, even during winter, to prepare the fire to cook for him. People believed

that having hot Before-Dawn Rice was good for the body. He would eat, then go back to sleep. I had to go on working to prepare the morning meal for him and his other wife. Sometimes I got so tired I would fall asleep in the kitchen. For sixty years, I have bought, prepared and cooked food, and made snacks and soup. I used to make different types of congee and soup for the family as the seasons changed. They never ate the leftovers, but I did. Maybe it's the best part, because these days my body is still healthy except for the occasional mild arthritis. I still spend a lot of time in the kitchen cooking for my beloved children and relatives. My husband is ninety now. He's in a wheelchair and needs to be looked after. He cares about me a lot.

In the older days, residents of a town would patrol the streets at night to guard against thieves and robbers. There were five shifts. Every shift was two hours, and drums and gongs were sounded. "Before-dawn" was the fifth shift, meaning 3am to 5am.

黑芝麻糕

黑芝麻300克
馬蹄粉600克
碎冰糖750克
紅棗2粒
清水12杯
椰汁1小罐（165 ml）

1 芝麻洗淨炒香，與兩杯清水一起放入攪拌機內磨成芝麻水，用隔渣布隔芝麻渣
2 中火煮滾芝麻水，放入碎冰糖，完全溶解後，待涼
3 用其餘清水溶解馬蹄粉，要邊加水邊攪，再加入椰汁攪勻
4 慢慢倒下芝麻水，攪勻
5 輕抹油在糕盆內側，倒入粉漿（倒入前記得要攪勻）*
6 水滾後，隔水以大火蒸約1小時，記著要不時在鑊邊加熱水，以防水燒乾，但不可揭蓋
7 蒸熟後，取出用冷水沖一沖糕盆底部，冷卻後反置碟上
8 放紅棗在芝麻糕上

* 亦可以做芝麻千層糕，只要將材料逐層倒入糕盆內，每次蒸3分鐘便成

Black Sesame Pudding

300 g black sesame
600 g water chestnut powder
750 g crushed rock sugar
2 red dates
12 cups water
1 bottle (165 ml) coconut paste

1 Rinse black sesame and fry at a low heat until fragrant. Put in blender with 2 cups of water and blend. Strain through a muslin cloth.
2 Boil strained sesame mixture in medium heat. Add crushed rock sugar. When melted, set aside and let cool.
3 Dissolve water chestnut powder with remaining water; pour and stir at the same time. Add in coconut paste. Mix and stir.
4 Slowly pour in sesame mixture. Stir well.
5 Grease inside of pudding pan. Pour mixture in. Remember to stir well before pouring in.*
6 Bring water to a boil in a big wok. On high heat, put pudding pan over boiling water and steam for about an hour. Remember to add hot water along the rim of wok from time to time to avoid water from drying up; do not uncover lid.
7 When done, remove pudding pan and run the bottom of pan with cold water. When cool, turn upside down on to a plate.
8 Put red dates on top of pudding.

** Turn this recipe into Thousand-layer Sesame Cake by pouring ingredients into the pudding pan layer by layer; steaming each layer for 3 mins.*

五更飯（有味飯）

白米及清水各1杯
雞肉40克（切粒）
冬菇2粒（切碎）
腰果6-8粒（切碎）
玉豆粒（或青菜切碎）及米酒各1湯匙
薑蓉2茶匙
油、糖、豉油各適量

1 冬菇粒以油、糖、豉油及薑蓉醃好備用
2 飯開始滾，下上述材料、腰果碎及雞肉粒
3 水乾後下玉豆，再焗數分鐘
4 最後下豉油及米酒

早飯又稱五更飯，是最經濟的補品，虛不受補者及產婦最宜於早上以飯為早餐。如胃口不振，可加梅菜粒及米酒同焗飯，有驅寒功效

Before-Dawn Rice (Tasty Rice)

1 cup each long-grain rice and water
40 g chicken fillet, diced
2 pieces winter mushroom, diced
6-8 pieces raw cashew nuts, diced
1 tbsp each green peas or chopped green vegetables and white rice wine
2 tsp minced ginger
some oil, sugar and soy sauce

1 Marinate diced mushrooms in oil, sugar, soy sauce and minced ginger. Set aside.
2 Boil the rice. When it starts bubbling, add mushrooms, raw cashew nuts and diced chicken.
3 When the water in the rice has boiled away, add green peas. Keep the cover on for a few mins.
4 Add soy sauce and rice wine to taste.

Before-dawn or morning rice is an economical tonic. It's good for those who are weak and women who have just given birth. For the latter, add diced fermented cabbage and rice wine to help keep the body warm.

電話還沒有普及，都得靠接線生接駁。

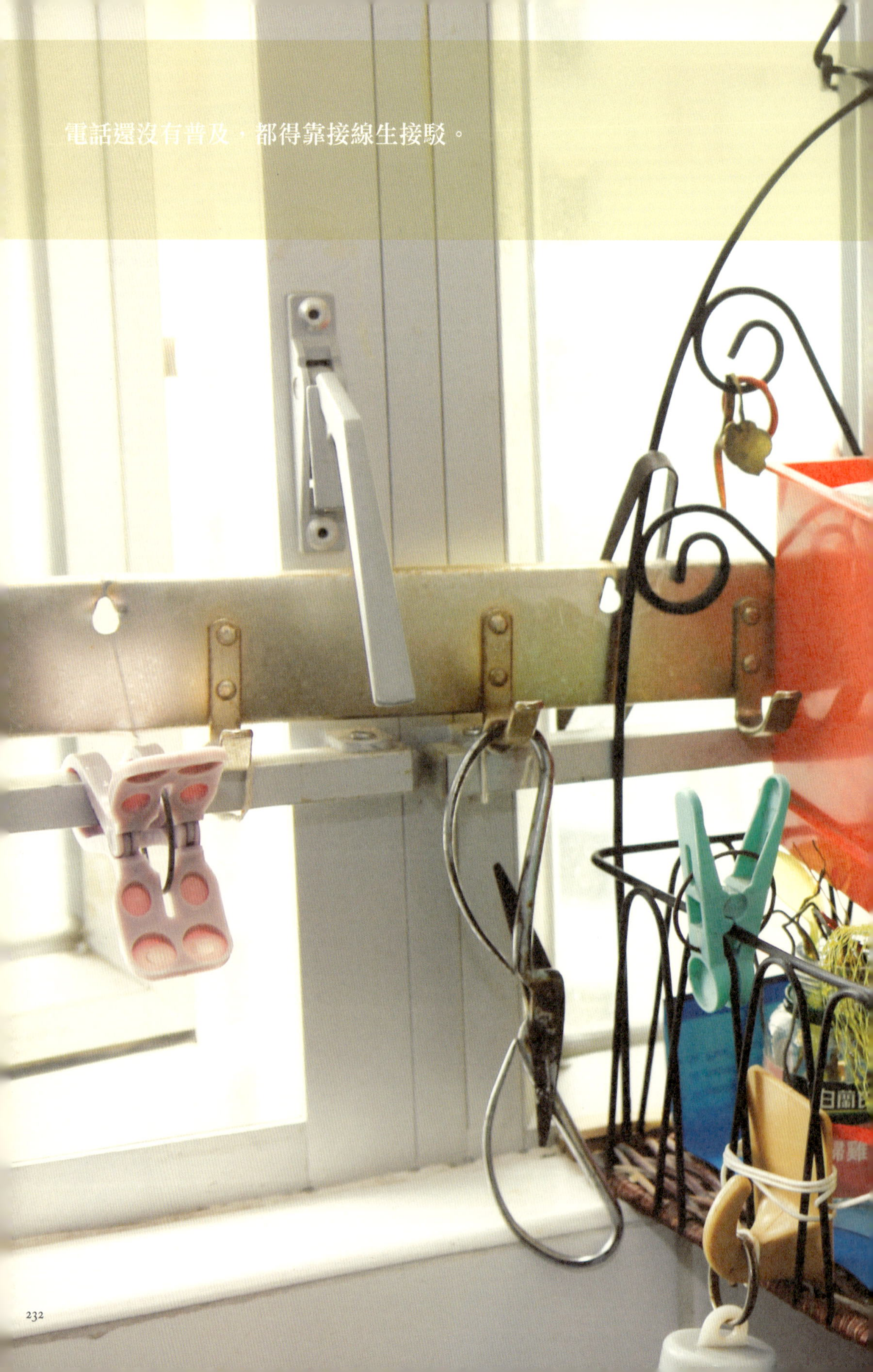

The telephone wasn't very common at that time.
If you wanted to call someone,
you needed to get the help of an operator.

周華英 八十三歲 祖籍上海

二十多歲時，我獨自到上海投靠親戚。文化大革命後去做「里弄工」，負責接線生的工作；那時電話還沒有普及，人們要找家人朋友時，都得靠接線生做接駁。我記得那時候的電話費大概每三分鐘五分錢。沒做接線生之後，我便在姨媽的家裡幫忙。照顧五個孩子之外，還得幫忙做家務，和到姨媽姨丈開的小店去幫忙。那裡賣的是生活必需品，柴米油鹽之類。有時候工廠要找替工，我也會幫上好一陣忙。1989年來港，很快便在製衣廠裡找到工作，負責剪線頭。雖然生活有點艱難，但有清茶淡飯和三餐溫飽，我已很滿足了。在上海的時候，醺魚和醺肉是常吃的食物，我卻最喜歡介紹朋友吃【上海炒年糕】，因為製作簡單而且材料豐富，一家大小都愛吃。另一款我喜愛的上海菜是【糯米丸子】。做法跟湯丸差不多，不過它是由糯米包裹著餡料。愛甜的可以用豆沙餡，愛鹹的用鹹肉或者其他肉類。糯米丸子甚至可以當正餐，是我在上海愛吃的食物之一啊。

I went to Shanghai when I was twenty to live with my relatives and find work. After the Cultural Revolution [1966-1976], I worked as a telephone operator. The telephone wasn't very common at that time. If you wanted to call someone, you needed to get the help of an operator. I remember the fee was about five cents for every three minutes. Later, I left

to work for my aunt, taking care of her five children at her home. Besides doing housework, I would help in her little shop, too. It was a cooperative my aunt and uncle opened. They sold daily necessities like wood, rice, oil and salt. Sometimes I worked part-time at the factory. I spent almost fifty years in Shanghai, and I came to Hong Kong in 1989. I quickly found a job at a garment factory. I worked as a seamstress. It was a little tight, but just filling my stomach with tea and rice was good. When I was in Shanghai, I always had smoked fish and smoked meat. But I like Fried Shanghai Glutinous Rice Pudding the most. It is easy to make and everyone loves it. I also love Glutinous Rice Balls. It's like the Guangdong Rice Balls, but the wrap is made of glutinous rice. If you like sweet things, you can put in mashed red bean paste. If you like it to be salty, you can use salted meat or something like that. These rice balls can also be the main dish.

糯米丸子

糯米2杯
豬肉250克
蝦乾1湯匙
白菜葉2片
紅蘿蔔半個（切花件）
胡椒粉、鹽、麻油、豉油、豆粉、酒，薑及葱適量

1 糯米洗淨，提前半小時用水泡一下，水剛浸過米即可
2 瀝乾水分，把糯米放於大碗中
3 肉和蝦乾剁碎，放入切碎了的薑、葱，拌勻
4 放入酒、豉油、鹽，豆粉等調味料、拌勻
5 用手擠出差不多大小的圓球形肉碎，然後放到糯米裡滾一下，讓肉丸表面沾上糯米，看來像「珍珠」
6 把刷上油的白菜葉及紅蘿蔔平放碟上。把「珍珠」丸子放在白菜和紅蘿蔔上。燒水，隔水蒸20分鐘即成

糯米丸子是用米做菜的典型案例，用糯米和豬肉或者其他餡料搭配而成，如魚肉或蝦肉，其做法應是來源於傳統湯圓，但是這道菜裡丸子的個頭就大了很多。用米把瘦肉包起來，團成丸子，上籠屜蒸20分鐘。成品的糯米丸子又圓又白，米粒一層層裹在外面，如同顆顆飽滿的珍珠，既可當菜又可當主食來吃。

Glutinous Rice Balls

2 cups glutinous rice
250 g pork
1 tbsp dried shrimp
2 leaves of *pak choi* / Chinese cabbage
half carrot sliced
pepper, salt, sesame oil, soy sauce, cornstarch and rice wine
spring onion

1 Rinse glutinous rice. Cover rice with water and soak half an hour before preparing dish. Drain and leave rice in a big bowl.
2 Mince meat. It's better to chop roughly by hand than to mince in a blender, which makes it less tasty and chewy.
3 Add in chopped ginger and spring onion before seasoning.
4 Put in some wine, soy sauce, salt and a small quantity of flour.
5 Knead mixture into round balls of approximately the same size. Roll into the bowl of glutinous rice so as to coat the meat balls with these glutinous "pearls".
6 Wash leaves and rub top with oil. Lay leaves on a plate.Place the pearls on top of the cabbage leaves and sliced carrots. Steam over boiling water for 20 minutes. When you smell the fragrance of the pearls and the light aroma of cabbage leaves, this dish is done.

Glutinous Rice Balls is a typical example of a dish using glutinous rice and pork or other fillings to complement one another. The recipe originates from traditional rice dumplings,but in this particular dish, the meat balls are comparatively larger in size. This dim sum simply wraps meat balls with glutinous rice and then steams over water for 20 minutes. The cooked glutinous rice balls are round and white–resembling round and full pearls.

上海炒年糕

上海年糕6條（浸軟切片）
紹菜300克（洗淨切絲）
冬菇2朵（浸軟去蒂切絲）
冬筍100克（撕去外衣切絲）
瑤柱2粒（浸軟撕碎）
肉100克（切絲）
榨菜2片（切絲）
上湯半杯，油1湯匙

1 肉絲用少許鹽和胡椒粉略醃
2 用油爆香肉絲後，加入其他配料，年糕放面（不要兜勻）
3 蓋上鍋蓋焗5分鐘
4 揭蓋後兜炒，若汁太多可調高火力，煮乾水分

上海年糕必須先用水浸軟，然後炒到軟硬適中，口感煙韌，才算成功。

Fried Shanghai Glutinous Rice Pudding

6 pieces Shanghai glutinous rice pudding (soak until soft; cut into thin slices)
300 g long cabbage, wash and shred
2 winter mushrooms, soak until soft; remove heads
100 g winter bamboo shoot
2 pieces dried scallop (soaked and shredded)
100 g meat (sliced)
2 pieces salted Szechuan vegetable
½ cup clear broth and 1 tbsp oil

1 Marinade shredded meat with some salt and pepper.
2 In hot oil, sauté shredded meat, put in remaining ingredients with sliced pudding on top. Do not stir-fry.
3 Cook for 5 minutes with cover.
4 Remove cover and stir-fry. Set to higher heat if there is too much sauce. Serve when sauce dries up.

Shanghai Glutinous Rice Pudding must be soaked until soft; then fry until the texture is just right (not too hard, not too soft). The taste is best if the pudding feels chewy.

回鄉後，轉行在街邊擺檔賣涼茶。

Without work, I had to go to the Mainland.
I started selling herbal tea on the streets.

林瓊　八十三歲　祖籍新會江門

想當年由鄉下葵涌到澳門，跟著二家姐生活，還需要什麼擔保費，足足二十塊！幸好我的叔叔替我付了。幾個月後，我就在太古船塢的太古大廈找了一份住家工。當時打住家工是沒有人工的，甚至過年也沒有特別零錢。可是僱主對我很好，如同家人一般。我不懂燒飯，所以主要負責擔水、洗衣服和照顧孩子。家裡沒有自來水，就要到街外打水，我每天都要走到街外公共水喉輪水。日本仔打到來，僱主辭退了我。沒有工作，唯有返鄉下。回鄉後，轉行在街邊擺檔賣涼茶。我們賣的涼茶沒有太多選擇，都是很簡單的，就是【狗肝菜糖水】。1958年，我走難到香港。起初賣五金，後來轉行做車衣，過了一段時間，由於腳痛再加上腰骨痛，醫生建議我做手術。1989年便停止車衣的工作。手術後，當時住在牛頭角，每天要走一段又長又斜的路才能回家。親戚便建議我跟他們到澳洲一起住，於是在澳洲住了幾年。始終也是不習慣，人生路不熟，不懂講英語，好像又盲又聾又啞似的。還是住在香港比較方便，儘管走那條斜路偶然會腳痛。在香港通常會吃什麼？中國人當然是吃飯嘛！我不太懂烹飪，對食物沒有太大要求，什麼食物都吃。丈夫卻比較喜歡吃蔬菜，除了撻沙魚外便不愛吃其他魚了，我也不知道為什麼。一家六口，兩兒兩女都長大了，全搬了出去住，偶然會一家人一起吃飯。我不愛搓麻將，空餘時就是買菜和晨運。以前沒有地鐵，又沒有隧道，乘小巴排隊也要一個多小時，一天很快就過了，哪裡有空餘時間培養什麼興趣！最開心的事，是當年有機會住廉租屋，再不用排隊打水、爭廁所，又有獨立廚房，多麼好！

所謂的「打住家工」，即今天我們的家庭傭工。那時僱主通常會包傭工的伙食，甚至住宿，所以有的僱主不一定給傭工發薪水。

It was a long time ago. I left my home in Kwai Chung to stay with my second sister in Macau. I had to pay a guarantee fee. It was some twenty dollars! Fortunately, my uncle helped me out. After a few months, I found work as a domestic helper with a family in the Taikoo shipyard back in Hong Kong. At that time, domestic

helpers did not have an income. There wasn't even pocket money for the Chinese New Year, but they treated me very well. I didn't know how to cook, so I was responsible for carrying water, washing clothes and taking care of the children. There was no tap in the house. We had to fetch water from the street. Every day, I had to queue up at the public taps. When the Japanese came, the family stopped employing me. Without work, I had to go to the Mainland. I started selling Chinese herbal tea on the streets. It was simply *kau kon choi* (Dicliptera) with sugar. When the communists came to power, I fled to Hong Kong. At first, I sold metal tools and parts. Then I turned to making clothes. After many years, I started getting pain in my feet and waist, and had to have an operation. Eventually, I stopped working as a seamstress. After the operation, I went to live in Ngau Tau Kok. The happiest thing for me was that the housing was cheap, and we didn't have to queue for water or fight to use the toilet. We even had our own kitchen. It was great! However, every day I had to walk up a long, steep slope to get home. My relatives suggested that I go and live with them in Australia. I went there for a few years, but couldn't get used to it. I was an outsider and couldn't speak English. It was as if I was deaf, dumb and blind. It's better in Hong Kong, even though the slope hurts my feet. What do we eat in Hong Kong? Rice, of course—we're Chinese! I don't cook well and I don't demand much from food. I can eat anything. My husband likes vegetables—and he only eats *tat sha* fish. I don't know why. There are six of us in the family. We have two sons and two daughters. They're all grown up now and live on their own. Occasionally, we eat together. When I have time, I shop at the market and do morning exercises. Before there was the Mass Transit Railway, waiting for a mini-bus took a whole hour. A day passed by quickly, so there was no time for hobbies.

狗肝菜糖水

狗肝菜60-100克
冰糖150克
水4杯
薑1片

1 狗肝菜洗淨，摘葉備用
2 燒熱水，加入薑及狗肝菜，煮至出味
3 加入冰糖，煮至糖溶便可食用

加入一小撮米同煮，便成為糖水粥，有清熱功效

Dicliptera Herb Sweet Soup

60 - 100 g dicliptera
150 g rock sugar
4 cups water
1 slice ginger

1 Wash the dicliptera; pick the leaves and set aside.
2 Bring water to a boil. Add in ginger and herbs and cook until fragrant.
3 Add in rock sugar. When sugar melts, then serve.

This dish becomes sweet congee by cooking together with a small handful of rice. It is good for reducing body heat.

那時菜田叫作瓜地，什麼也有種。
耕田的人種什麼就吃什麼。

Our family had farmland
called squash fields, and fish ponds.
We grew everything we needed.

周蝶　七十七歲　家鄉南海

解放後我便由內地來港，已有五十多年了。現在回家鄉也認不出老地方，因為那兒發展得太快了。在家鄉的幾個姐妹，生活都比在香港的我好。七兄弟姐妹中，我最大。由於家境不錯，家裡的工作都有伙計做，所以阿爺從來不用小孩子做家務。我結婚以後，才親力親為打理家頭細務。小時候生活無憂無慮，阿爺説讀書沒有用，於是我每天就到處玩。我們小孩子的遊戲很簡單，有時會用禾稈草扭成繩來玩，有時將拾來的瓦片磨滑了來拋，但都不及和朋友一起爬桑樹摘桑果吃快樂。最頑皮要算是走到蔗田，跟朋友在每條蔗上咬上一口，然後告訴父親那是老鼠咬的，他竟然相信呢。玩厭了，便想快點出來工作。後來便跟親戚來香港學織布。那時看見人家沒飯吃，只是吃雞糠、花生枯和番薯，吃得頭腫面腫。於是，我在家盛了一大碗白飯，拿給人家，叫他把手上的番薯換給我，之後再回家添「大鑊飯」換給人家。至於換回來的番薯怎麼辦？都給了豬吃。慶幸家裡有田有地還有魚塘，那時菜田叫作瓜地，什麼也有種。耕田的人種什麼就吃什麼，下田工作的伙計，通常會吃幾餐，包括早飯、午飯、三點和晚飯。三點就像我們現在的下午茶，多數吃粥粉或煎薄餅。家鄉物資富庶，最多是竹筍，竹筍可以有多種吃法，例如可以拌豉油或熟油，也可灑上胡椒粉來吃。【竹筍釀魚肉】這個菜的做法就像釀茄子一樣，很容易的呢。

五六十年代，中國奉行社會主義，在各農村成立「人民公社」。公社為農民安排衣食住行，農民所有生產由國家計劃及統一收購，農民所需的商品則由國家分配。當時並設有公共食堂，不論食堂大小，每個社員均得吃飽，以大鍋提供伙食，便於生產，吃飯時間亦統一。

It's been fifty years since I arrived in Hong Kong from the mainland. Now, when I go back to my hometown, I hardly recognize the place. It has developed so quickly. My sisters there now have a higher standard of living than I do. I'm the eldest of seven brothers and sisters. My family was well off and we had many helpers. My grandfather never let children do housework.

Life was so carefree when I was young. Grandfather said there was no use studying at school, so I played all day. We played simple games: sometimes, we twisted straw into ropes; sometimes we picked up broken pieces of china, ground them up and threw them. I loved climbing trees and picking mulberries to eat. Sometimes, we were very naughty and went into the sugar cane fields and bit into every single stick of cane. My father actually believed me when I told him they were rat bites! Then I got bored and wanted to start working. So, as soon as I was old enough, I followed a relative to Hong Kong to learn weaving. Some years were very hard for the local people. I remember seeing people with no rice to eat—only chicken feed, dried peanuts or sweet potatoes. Their faces and heads would swell up badly. I got so upset that I sometimes took a big bowl of rice from home and gave it to people in exchange for their sweet potato. I would go back and get more rice to fill their big rice pan. What did I do with the sweet potatoes? I gave them to the pigs. Our family had farmland called squash fields, and fish ponds. We grew everything we needed. The workers who went into the fields would have several meals a day: breakfast, lunch, "three o'clock" in the afternoon and dinner. "Three o'clock" is what we call "afternoon tea" now. They usually had congee, rice noodles or pancakes. There were plenty of bamboo shoots in our hometown. There are many ways of preparing them—for instance, you can dip them in soy sauce or oil and sprinkle them with pepper. Stuffed Bamboo Shoots with Fish is like stuffed eggplant. It's very easy to make.

"Big rice pan" is a phrase used in socialist China during the 1950s and 1960s to mean communal meals for peasants provided by the state. Each village had a "people's commune" which organized the daily lives of peasants.

竹筍釀魚肉

鮮竹筍150克
冬菇40克
鯪魚肉70克
薑片1-2片
紅蘿蔔數片
醃料：糖、生粉各1/4茶匙，鹽1/8茶匙，酒1茶匙
調味：麵豉醬1茶匙，上湯1杯，糖1/2茶匙，鹽、胡椒粉、麻油各少許，生粉適量

1 冬菇浸軟去蒂，加入醃料，拌勻備用
2 鯪魚肉*加入少許糖、鹽、胡椒粉、麻油，拌勻，攪至起膠，備用
3 鮮竹筍削去厚皮，只要最鮮嫩的筍肉，放入沸水中煮約15分鐘，取出用冷水沖洗，抹乾水分，切厚片
4 在厚片竹筍中間切一刀，不要切斷，成雙飛狀的竹筍夾
5 在竹筍夾內抹上生粉，並釀入適量的魚肉，泡油，撈出，瀝乾油分
6 於鑊中放少許油，爆香麵豉醬，將竹筍夾子回鑊，加入冬菇、上湯、糖、鹽及紅蘿蔔煮滾，改慢火煮約20分鐘至汁收乾，便可上碟

* 可按個人喜好，在魚肉內加入蔥粒、蝦米粒或薑粒等材料

Stuffed Bamboo Shoots with Fish

150 g fresh bamboo shoots
40 g winter mushrooms
70 g minced fish, daced
1-2 slices ginger
few slices carrot
marinade : ¼ tsp each sugar and cornstarch, 1/8 tsp salt, 1 tsp cooking wine
seasoning : 1 tsp Chinese miso paste, 1 cup stock, ½ tsp sugar, salt, pepper and sesame oil to taste cornstarch for dusting
8 tbsp oil

1 Soak mushrooms until soft and remove stems. Add the marinade and mix well.
2 In a separate bowl, add sugar, salt, pepper and sesame oil to the minced dace* and mix well. Stir until it becomes glutinous.
3 Remove the thick skin from the bamboo shoots, so only the most tender part is left. Cook in boiling water for about 15 minutes, then rinse with cold water. Wipe dry and cut into thick slices.
4 Make a cut along each slice without cutting through, forming a sandwich shape.
5 Dust the inside of each slice with cornstarch. Stuff bamboo shoots with minced dace. Heat 8 tbsps of oil in a wok and cook slices for about 30 seconds. Drain.
6 Heat oil in a clean wok and stir-fry the miso paste until fragrant. Add stuffed bamboo shoots first, then mushrooms, stock, sugar, carrots and salt. Bring to a boil, then simmer for about 20 minutes until the sauce thickens. Serve immediately.

** According to taste, add chopped spring onions, finely diced dried shrimps or chopped ginger to the minced dace.*

每一件衣服也相當寶貴。
以我家為例，每人只有三件衣服……

Those were difficult days. Even just one outfit was very precious.
In my family, each one of us had three outfits.

侯麗棠　七十四歲　祖籍新會

我的父親是「Fit 打」，亦可說是「船頭官」，那是當時對在海事處做事的人的稱呼。我父親十多歲就跟鄉里來香港工作，在西營盤直接跟著一位西人上司做有關機器的工作。日軍進佔香港期間，我只有七、八歲。有一天，父親的西人上司被日軍捉了作俘虜，卻不知怎的這個西人竟然逃脫了，於是父親被日軍捉了去問話。這一問，足足把父親關了一個月。我當時年紀小，家人只告訴我父親去了燈塔工作，他回來後，我才知道真相。我想父親當時一定受過不好的對待，但為免我們擔心，所以在我們面前絕口不提。父親回來後繼續在海事處做事，謹守崗位，一直做到退休。父親在外頭工作，十歲左右的我就跟著母親在家學做家務。由於當時香港仍有點亂，年輕女子都盡量避免走上街，不幸的話隨時會被日軍捉去做花姑娘。我年紀雖小但膽子大，經常幫忙到街上拿配給品，可是始終因為年紀小，我還是多次被騙去食物。更有一次，當母親上了街，剩我一人在家，一位陌生人摸上門，說是我父母的朋友。我就讓他進來坐坐。怎料街上突然響起防空警報，為免受到炮彈碎片的傷害，我馬上隨鄰居跑到大廈樓梯底去躲避。警報完後回到家，卻發覺那陌生人走了，而母親的一件衣服不見了，結果被母親狠狠地責罵了一頓。那時生活艱難，每一件衣服也是相當寶貴。以我家為例，每人只有三件衣服，一件是穿來「上街」的，即是在特別日子或大時大節才會穿著，其餘兩件就是平常替換的，所以對窮苦大眾來說，失了一件衣服已是很大的損失。不似現在的人，衣服還沒有破爛就要買新的了。我常常提醒兒孫要減少物慾，珍惜已擁有的東西。另外，我最記得的就是母親做的【狗仔粥】和【雞屎藤茶果】。「狗仔粥」最特別之處，是母親將生米磨成米漿後，混和冷飯和上湯做成的，雖然材料簡單，卻盡顯心思和創意。雞屎藤茶果除了是清熱祛濕的小吃，也是我的童年回憶。至於孫兒最愛吃的則是【珠圓玉潤魷魚快樂豬肉餅】，雖然媳婦也曾跟我學做這個菜，可是依樣做出來後，孫兒仍然嚷著我這個祖母做的才是最好吃的呢。

雞屎藤，蔓藤類植物，通常生長於氣候溫和潮濕的地方，生命力強。揉爛其葉，會有股雞屎味，曬乾後反會滲出陣陣清香。有藥用價值，可清熱、解毒、祛濕、補血，所以又名「土參」。

I had been through the war, and I remember it as memories of my father. He came to Hong Kong with his friends from the same province when he was ten years old. He worked at the Marine Department at Sai Ying Pun as what they called a 'fitter'. He worked for a Western boss on mechanical things. People called my father 'civil servant at the ship's

mass'. When the Japanese came, I was about seven. One day, my father's boss was captured by the Japanese but escaped somehow. The Japanese came and took my father away for interrogation. He was imprisoned for over a month. I was too small. All my family told me was he went to work at a lighthouse. I learned what happened when he came back. I think my father must have had a bad time, but he didn't want us to worry so he kept quiet about it. I admire my father a lot. He went back to work at the Marine Department until he retired. When father was working, I tailed behind my mother at home and learned to do housework. It was still an unstable time. It would be dangerous for young women to go out on the streets because the Japanese might capture them to become flower ladies. When going out to get food rations—only a few times—I would get cheated. I remember one day, my mother went out and I was alone at home. A stranger came knocking at the door and claimed he was a friend of my parents. I let him come into the house. Suddenly, an alarm went off. I was afraid of the bombs so I ran to hide under the stairs in the building with my neighbours. When it was over, I went back home. The stranger was gone, and my mother's only nice outfit was also gone. My mother scolded me fiercely. Those were difficult days. Even just one outfit was very precious. In my family, each one of us had three outfits. One was for going out (that means for use on special days or festivals). The other two were for ordinary days. For common people like us, losing one outfit was a big loss. People are so wasteful nowadays! They buy new clothes when the old ones are still good. I always remind my grandchildren to cherish what they have. About food, I like "puppy congee" that my mother made a lot. She ground the rice into a paste, combined that with cooked rice leftovers and stock and made congee. The ingredients were simple but it was very creative. Fevervine Herbs *Cha Guo* was for purging the heat and humidity in the body. My grandchildren like pork cake. My daughter-in-law tries to make it too, but they still like mine.

When fevervine herbs leaves are mashed, they give out a stench like chicken droppings, which is why they are known as "chicken droppings herb" in Chinese. After being sun-dried, they become fragrant. They are also nutritious.

雞屎藤茶果

糯米粉240克
熟麵粉40克（麵粉與熱開水各20克混成）
雞屎藤汁液140克
糖60克
油1湯匙
竹葉數片
餡料：白芝麻40克（炒香），花生碎、椰絲、糖各80克

1 洗淨竹葉，剪成方塊，上少許油，待用
2 將糯米粉、熟麵粉、糖混合，加入雞屎藤汁液*及油拌勻
3 搓成軟滑之粉糰，分成若干等份，壓成小圓塊作粉皮
4 混合所有餡料
5 每個粉皮加入適量餡料，捏好，排放在竹葉上，輕壓成圓餅形
6 放入蒸籠，蒸8-10分鐘

* 可用抹茶粉2茶匙，加入約140克清水攪勻代替雞屎藤汁

Fevervine Herb Cha Guo

240 g glutinous rice flour
40 g cooked flour
(mix 20 g of flour with 20 g of boiling water)
140 g fevervine herb extract*
60 g sugar
several sheets bamboo leaves
1 tbsp oil
filling ingredients : 40 g fried white sesame, 80 g each crushed fried peanut, desiccated coconut shreds and sugar

1 Rinse bamboo leaves, cut into squares, and spread surface with a little oil.
2 Mix glutinous rice flour, cooked flour and sugar. Add in herb extract and oil, mix thoroughly.
3 Knead mixture into dough; divide into equal portions of small balls and roll flat to form wraps.
4 Mix all filling ingredients.
5 Put on appropriate amount of fillings into each wrap, fold up and display neatly on top of bamboo leaves. Press lightly shape.
6 Steam over a steaming pot for 8-10 minutes. Serve.

** Fevervine herb extract can be substituted by a mixture of 2 tbsps of green tea powder and 140g of water.*

珠圓玉潤魷魚快樂豬肉餅

枚頭肉190克（約5兩）
半乾濕吊片1隻
蔥花少許
豉油、生粉、鹽及糖適量

1 洗淨半乾濕吊片，切幼粒
2 洗淨枚頭肉*，抹乾，切成薄片，再切成幼絲，然後切成幼粒，可輕剁數下
3 於豬肉內下1茶匙生粉，拌勻，並將肉撻數下，使其有黏性
4 加入吊片粒，豉油、鹽、糖等調味，拌勻，放碟中，灑上蔥花
5 大火隔水蒸15分鐘，便可食用

* 宜選擇較嫩且肥瘦適中的豬肉

Happy Pearly Steamed Pork Cake with Dried Squid

190 g lean pork*
1 palm-size semi-dried squid
some chopped spring onion, soy sauce, cornstarch, salt and sugar

1 Wash and soak dried squid and dice into small pieces.
2 Rinse and wipe dry the pork. Cut into thin slices. Shred and dice, then chop a few times.
3 Mix pork in a bowl with 1 tsp of cornstarch. Scoop it up and slap it back into the bowl. Mix and repeat until the mash becomes sticky.
4 Add diced squid, soy sauce, salt and sugar. Mix well. Put the mixture on a plate and sprinkle with chopped spring onion.
5 Steam over boiling water for 15 minutes and serve.

** Tender and semi-fatty lean pork is best.*

見到那些活生生的禾蟲在蜷縮，
嚇得我不敢走近。

When I saw the grain worms wriggling,
I wouldn't dare go near them.

十歲左右，日本仔來的時候，無得食啊！父親帶我們走難來香港。和平後，物資還是缺乏，難得有一餐肉吃，那時爸爸蒸的肥豬肉餅，就是人間美食。其實走難時吃的食物也挺有趣。走難到澳門，外婆見我們無得食，就給我們煮「大媽地」。「大媽地」其實是番茄的葡文讀法。我最喜歡外婆用「大媽地」跟滑溜溜的九肚魚一起煮，就是【大媽地煮魚】。外婆還有一個小風爐，可以用來自製【炒米餅】。她會先磨好炒米粉，放進餡料，再用餅模壓成餅，最後用小風爐烤出陣陣香味，可惜我現在沒有牙，已經不能吃炒米餅了！還有禾蟲，初時我見到就怕怕。父親就很愛吃，更會親自下廚炒禾蟲。當時我八、九歲，見到那些活生生的禾蟲在蜷縮，嚇得我不敢走近。後來見到父親吃得很滋味，才壯起膽來試，想不到一試便愛上了。之後父親每次煮禾蟲，我都會幫忙剪禾蟲，蠻有趣的。香港現在禁止入口禾蟲，所以每當有朋友到澳門旅遊，我定會託他們買些禾蟲，回味一番。始終很懷念那沒有嘗過肉味的歲月，我就從父親那裡偷學了這味蒸肉餅。枚頭肉自己剁才好吃，不要太肥也不可以太瘦，那樣才算鮮嫩，千萬不能放味精，要保留鮮肉味，若果有多些肥豬肉就更香口。今天在外邊很多地方都可以吃到這味簡單的蒸肉餅，但餐廳弄出來的總是放了味精，不然就是缺少鮮肉味，總是差一點！母親去世後，爸爸娶來後母，就沒有再弄這肥豬肉餅了。當年我們還是孩子時都會爭吃肥肉，現在的孩子自然不肯吃肥肉。在肉餅加入吊片和馬蹄，就更惹味。也許是經過打仗無肉吃的日子，突然試到肉味，就感到非同凡響！孩子現在回家，常問我幾時會蒸肉餅。今時今日吃肉的機會雖多，但孩子最愛吃的仍是這簡單的蒸肉餅。味道總算遺傳下來。

禾蟲多棲身於稻田表土層，以禾根為食，通體粉紅，含有豐富蛋白質和維生素。蒸炒煲炖焗均可，美味異常，有滋陰壯陽、健脾暖身、生血祛濕之效。自從農田施用農藥後，禾蟲數目驟減，現在吃到的多是人工養殖的。

When I was about ten, the Japanese came and there was nothing to eat. We fled to Hong Kong, staying first with my grandmother in Macau. She used to make us *dai ma dei* (tomatoes). I loved it when she cooked it with smooth, creamy Bombay duck fish. She also used to make Fried (Crispy) Rice Cookies on her small stove. She would grind the rice powder well,

Grain worms feed on weeds. Pink in colour, they are rich in protein and vitamins. They can be steamed, fried, stewed or baked. They are good for warming and strengthening the body. The use of chemical fertilizers in the fields has been damaging to their natural habitat. Most grain worms are now artificially bred.

put in the fillings, then mould the cookies and bake them. They gave out such an aroma! It's a pity I don't have the teeth for them now. In Hong Kong, there was often nothing to eat. To be able to have even one meal with meat was rare. There were grain worms, which my father would fry. At first, I was scared of them, but my father loved them. I would see the grain worms wriggling and I wouldn't go near them. One day, I mustered up my courage and tried some. I immediately fell in love with them! After that, whenever my father made them, I would help him. They were prohibited in Hong Kong, so whenever we had friends visiting Macau, we would ask them to bring some back. Funnily enough, I miss the days when we didn't have meat. The steamed fat pork that my father made in those days was absolutely heavenly. I used to watch him and learned how to make steamed pork cake. It's always better to dice the *mui tao* pork [pork belly] at home. It can't be too fat or too thin. Never use MSG, because it destroys the fresh taste of the meat. The fat makes it juicy. When we were kids, we would fight for the fat, but nowadays children refuse to eat it. We would add slices of squid and water chestnuts to sharpen the taste. After mother died, my father married another woman, and he stopped making steamed pork cake. Most restaurants that offer this dish nowadays put MSG in the meat. It's never as good as I think it should be. I've got good taste when it comes to meat—probably because of all those years during the war when we didn't have any. When my children come home nowadays, they always ask me to make steamed pork. Even though meat is so plentiful these days, they love this simple dish.

大媽地煮魚

紅衫魚1條（約450-600克）
番茄4個
洋蔥1個
薑4片
蒜頭2瓣
調味：酒1湯匙，胡椒粉1/8茶匙，上湯1 1/4杯，砂糖、生抽各1茶匙

1 用紙吸乾魚身，以油、鹽、胡椒粉醃，備用
2 番茄每個切成4份備用
3 洋蔥去衣，切絲備用
4 用刀背將蒜頭拍扁
5 薑兩片切絲備用
6 燒紅鑊下油，放入薑2片，把魚煎成金黃色，盛起候用
7 原鑊再燒紅，爆香蒜頭，下洋蔥略炒，加入番茄兜勻
8 將紅衫魚放回鑊內，下酒，加上湯*及調味料，煮5分鐘後上碟

* 可用清水代替上湯

Fried Golden Thread Fish with Tomatoes

1 golden thread fish (450 - 600 g)
4 tomatoes
1 onion
4 slices ginger
2 cloves garlic
seasonings : 1 tbsp rice wine, ⅛ tbsp pepper, 1 ¼ cups clear broth*, 1 tsp each granulated sugar and light soy sauce

1 Wash and clean fish. Wipe-dry. Marinade with pepper for 20 minutes. Set aside.
2 Cut each tomato into 4 slices. Set aside.
3 Skin onion and cut into shreds. Set aside.
4 Squash garlic with the back of chopping knife. Set aside.
5 Cut 2 slices of ginger into shreds. Set aside.
6 Heat wok with oil. Add in ginger and shallow fry fish until golden yellow on both sides. Transfer fish to a plate and set aside.
7 Sauté garlic, stir fry onion briefly, add tomato and other ingredients, mix well.
8 Return the fish to the wok, sprinkle wine, pour in clear broth and seasonings. Simmer for 5 minutes and dish on to a plate.

**As an alternative, use water.*

炒米餅

粘米粉、糖各320克
豬油120克
麵粉、水各40克
花生適量（壓碎、炒香）
餅模

1 豬油煮溶，加入糖拌勻，置鍋中數小時，待用
2 粘米粉、麵粉分別炒熟後，加入壓碎炒香的花生肉拌勻，再加入豬油與糖的混合物及水，搓透*
3 將混合物放餅模中，加壓成形後倒出，放入焗爐用170℃焗10分鐘後，改用150℃焗30分鐘，待涼後便可食用

* 可用糙米粉代替粘米粉。水分可因天氣變化而作適量之增減

Fried (Crispy) Rice Cookies

320 g each rice flour* and sugar
40 g each flour and water
120 g lard
some crushed fried peanuts

1 Melt lard, then mix in sugar. Leave to stand for a few hours. Set aside.
2 Fry rice flour and flour separately until cooked. Add crushed fried peanuts and mix well. Add to melted lard and sugar.
3 Pour into round cookie-baking mould, press firmly into the shapes and remove from mould. Set oven to 170°c and bake for 10 minutes. Reset to 150°c and bake for 30 minutes. Let cool and serve.

** Coarse rice flour can be substituted for rice flour.*

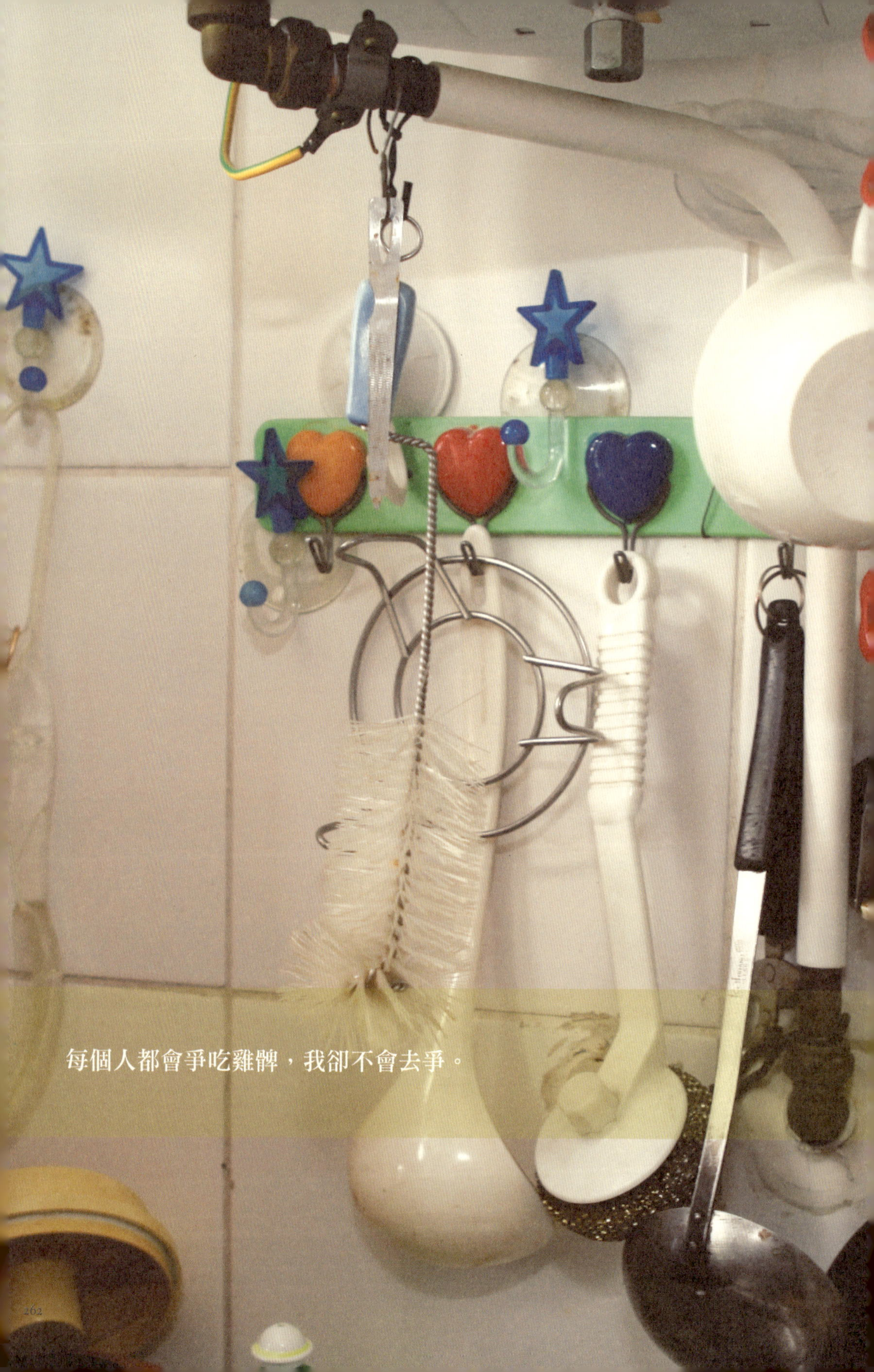

每個人都會爭吃雞髀，我卻不會去爭。

Everyone fought for the chicken legs,
but I could never get them.

游惠嫦　七十二歲　祖籍新會

我有兩個媽媽，十個兄弟姐妹。平日，兩個媽媽是分開住的，我們十兄弟姐妹跟著自己的生母。爸爸是做生意的，常要兩頭走，一時跟大媽住，一時跟二媽住，過年時一家人才會團聚。每逢做節，因為家族較大，弄十隻雞也不夠吃。每個人都會爭吃雞髀，我卻不會去爭，反而愛吃【蘿蔔魚肉燴肉絲】。我年紀小，人又多，雞髀就一定爭不贏了，燴肉絲這味每逢過節都會煮的菜，不用爭就可以吃，而且很好吃。每次都會因不去爭雞髀吃而被讚乖呢，絕對百利而無一害。幼時在鄉下居住，還未解放的時候，曾經有機會讀書，那時家有不少工人，我從來不須做家務。解放後，給共產黨清算，不要說讀書，連食也是個問題，有時更要姑姐寄錢來幫補。當時，姑姐在香港做清潔工作，我家則以賣葵扇為生。我家上下人多，食物不夠，每天只有將番薯混白米來煮，加一點鹽便是了。捱了好幾年辛苦的日子後，我便申請來香港，做製衣工作。初時，我寄居在姑姐家裡，後來跟幾個朋友合租一間房子住。一做便十年，然後結婚。丈夫本就是我的親戚，可是到港後我們才認識。婚後搬到灣仔，住在以前東方戲院的附近。那條走廊，在記憶中是很長很長的，走很久很久才到達廁所。我就常常跟丈夫去英京茶樓飲茶，現在大概拆了吧！我們是跟家婆一起住的，家婆負責煮飯，從不讓我進廚房，因那時候要燒柴，常常弄得很骯髒，我唯有幫手開飯洗碗。所以，我不懂得烹飪。婚後倒學會煮我最喜歡的蘿蔔魚肉燴肉絲，兒女也很愛吃，特別是蘿蔔。最好吃更是加入韭菜和鹹酸菜等配菜。那是道很有意頭的菜，「蘿蔔煮魚，齊齊團年」，在（中國）新年時煮就很有意思。

葵樹為棕櫚科亞熱帶常綠喬木，耐旱且耐濕，夏天比冬天生長更快。葉面寬大呈圓形，輕盈柔韌，多被加工製成葵扇。舊日電風扇和空調尚不太普遍，葵扇是尋常百姓家的生活必需品。

I have two mothers and ten brothers and sisters. My mothers lived separately, each with her own children. My father was a businessman. He used to dash between the two homes, sometimes staying with First Mother and sometimes with Second Mother. We ate together only during Chinese New Year, when we would have chicken. My

family was so big that even ten chickens could barely feed us all! Everyone fought for the chicken legs, but I was too young and there were so many of us, so I could never get them. Instead, I used to eat the Stewed Turnip and Clam with Pork Shreds. No one fought for this. And since I didn't fight for the chicken legs, I was always praised for being obedient. It all worked in my favour. We lived in a village when I was small. That was before the liberation in 1949. I used to go to school, but when the communists came, they launched purges. Not only could we not go to school, but we didn't even have enough to eat. Before the communists came, we had several helpers at home and I never had to do housework. Afterwards, there was little to eat. My father's sister sometimes sent us money from Hong Kong, where she was working as a cleaner for a family business that sold palm leaf fans. Most days, we ate rice blended with sweet potato—sometimes with a pinch of salt. Those were hard times. A few years later, I came to Hong Kong on my own and found work in a garment factory. At first, I lived with my aunt. Then I rented a room with a few friends. For the next ten years, until I got married, I sewed clothes. My husband was a distant relative, but I met him in Hong Kong. After we got married, we moved to an old building with his mother in Wan Chai, near the former Oriental Cinema. My mother-in-law did all the cooking and never let me in the kitchen because I made a mess burning firewood. So I helped set the table and do the dishes. Occasionally, we ate out. We used to have *dim sum* at the Ying King Chinese Restaurant. It's probably demolished now. I never learned how to cook properly because I never had to. However, I did learn how to make my favorite dish: Stewed Turnip and Clam with Pork Shreds. My children like it—especially the turnip. It's even better if you add chives or salted and sour cabbage. I call it "Turnip and Clam—Together We Join Hands". It's very meaningful when you cook it for Chinese New Year.

Palm leaves are drought and humidity resistant. Since the leaves are big and round, light and resilient, they are made into fans. In the old days, when electric fans and air conditioners were not common, palm leaf fans were essential objects in every home.

蜆肉蘿蔔絲魚鬆

蘿蔔一個（中）
蜆肉100克
魚肉200克
調味：酒、醬油、油各1湯匙，
魚上湯、清水各1杯，
中國芹菜1-2條，麻油、原粒胡椒、
薑、蔥花、蒜蓉適量

1. 魚肉加鹽、胡椒粉、麻油調味，攪拌至起膠
2. 燒紅鑊，下少量油，爆香薑、蒜蓉，將魚肉壓平放鑊中慢火煎，切長條備用。
3. 蘿蔔切段，加鹽，氽水備用
4. 水加酒、醬油、薑片、原粒胡椒，煮沸後放入蜆肉煮熟，盛起蜆肉，煮蜆汁留起待用
5. 慢火用蜆汁和魚上湯煮蘿蔔至腍軟*（約半小時）
6. 熟後拌入蜆肉、魚鬆及薑絲、蔥花，收火即可上碟

* 加入中國芹菜與蘿蔔同煮，味道更香

Stewed Turnip and Clam with Pork Shreds

1 medium-sized white turnip
100 g clam
200 g dace flesh
2 each ginger slices and cloves garlic
seasoning : 1 tbsp each soy sauce, rice wine, oil; 1 cup each fish broth and water; 1-2 stalks Chinese celery; some sesame oil, whole peppercorn, salt, ginger shreds and chopped spring onion

1. Season fish flesh with salt, pepper corn and sesame oil, and blend until sticky.
2. Heat wok with a little oil. Sauté ginger and minced garlic. Add fish flesh, press flat and fry on a medium-low heat. Cut into long slices and set aside.
3. Peel turnip, cut into sections and blanch in water. Drain and set aside.
4. Add water, wine, soy sauce and ginger slices. Bring to a boil. Add clam and cook until done. Set aside the cooked clam sauce.
5. Simmer turnip* in cooked clam sauce and fish broth until soft (about 30 minutes).
6. When cooked, mix in clam, minced fish and chopped spring onion. Remove from heat and serve.

* *Cooking the turnip with a few stalks of Chinese celery enhances the flavour of the dish.*

絕大部分技巧都是從李太和方太的烹飪節目中和書上慢慢學回來的。

I learned most of what I know from cooking programmes on television and from books.

陳惠卿　六十八歲　家鄉東莞

我是東莞石龍人，生於香港的四十年代。在十一個兄弟姊妹當中，我排行第五。約三歲的時候，我得了嚴重的百日咳，導致聽覺受損，說話也變得有困難。由於弱聽的關係，小時候沒有學校肯收我讀書，所以只好留在家，在媽媽和傭人身邊整天團團轉。後來家人請了老師回來教我讀書寫字，我也就學了兩、三年。從那時候開始，我學習做一些家務。但當時年紀小，媽媽不讓我進廚房，我只有靠觀察來學一點廚房工夫。到我需要親手烹飪的時候，人已長大，而絕大部分技巧都是從李太和方太的烹飪節目中和書上慢慢學回來的，某程度上算是無師自通吧。我一直沒有正式工作，閒時會去做義工。由於喜愛烹飪，我曾在佛堂協助煮齋菜，差不多十年了，最拿手的是齋叉燒和齋燒鴨。由於準備的分量要供應百多人食用，所以很需要人手。直到好幾年前我信了耶穌，便沒有再在佛堂裡做義工。我最愛看別人吃我的拿手小菜的樣子，尤其是我的兒子亞存。他小時候放學回家，我總會用一個小瓦煲準備一碗熱氣騰騰的【蝦乾瑤柱煲仔飯】給他，他會說：「這飯是天下最好的美食。」我就樂透了。我弄的蝦乾瑤柱煲仔飯材料並不複雜，最重要是用心去看火候，這才做出香口美味的飯焦。我用來做煲仔飯的瓦煲已有二十年歷史，但是我一直捨不得把它換掉，因為它對我來說有很特別的紀念價值。記得兒子讀中三的時候，大女兒正在讀預科。那一年，我患病進了醫院，女兒便買了這個小瓦煲，定時送飯菜給我。每次回想起，我都很感動，也很安慰，所以就算小瓦煲現在已經很少用，我還是把它保存起來，留為紀念。

現今流行無火煮食，可是曾為民間普遍採用的煮食用具——瓦煲，仍有不可取替的地位。瓦煲導熱慢，溫度均勻穩定，保溫時間長，加熱時湯汁氣化少，不含金屬異味，又能保菜餚原味，煲粥煮飯尤佳，煎中藥更是必備。

I'm the fifth of eleven children. When I was three, I developed whooping cough, which damaged my hearing and even made speaking difficult. No school would accept me, so I stayed at home. My parents hired a tutor who taught me to read and write for three years. I also learned to do some household chores, but because I was too young, my

mother wouldn't let me in the kitchen. I learned some things just by watching, but I didn't really learn to cook properly until I was grown up. I learned most of what I know from cooking programmes on television and from books. For about ten years, I helped cook vegetarian meals at a Buddhist hall. I had to prepare for more than one hundred people sometimes, so I had quite a few helpers. My best dishes were vegetarian roast pork and vegetarian roast duck. A few years ago, I converted to Christianity, so I stopped volunteering there. I like to see people eat what I cook—especially my son. I used to make him dried shrimp and scallop rice in a small, clay pot. When he came home from school, he would say, "This is the best food on earth and in heaven." I would be so delighted! The ingredients are simple. The important thing is to watch the heat so you get the best crust at the bottom of the pot. I've had the same pot for more than twenty years. When my son was in Form 3 and my daughter was in her final year, I fell ill and was hospitalized for a while. My daughter used to bring me rice and vegetables in this small clay pot every day. When I think about that, I get a wonderful warm feeling. We seldom use the pot now, but I keep it for the memories.

Clay pots are still widely used in an ordinary Chinese home. They transmit heat evenly, and there is no smell from metals. They are also good for making Chinese herbal medicine.

蝦乾瑤柱煲仔飯

米1杯
蝦乾數隻
瑤柱2粒
蛋1隻
醬汁：老抽2湯匙，薑汁、燒酒各1湯匙，糖1茶匙

1 瑤柱洗淨，加半杯水浸軟後，撕成幼絲，瑤柱水留用
2 蝦乾洗淨，加半杯水浸軟後，取出，蝦乾水留用
3 將米洗淨倒入瓦煲內，加入瑤柱水、蝦乾水，蓋上煲蓋
4 用猛火煲至水滾後，放入蝦乾，改用慢火
5 煲至差不多飯熟時，下瑤柱絲
6 飯熟透後，熄火再焗15分鐘
7 蛋打開，加在飯面，焗熟後淋上醬汁，便可食用

煲底飯焦可加上湯、醃菜煮成泡飯，甘香味美

鳴謝：簡梁以瑚女士提供菜式及烹調方法

Dried Shrimp & Scallop Rice in Clay Pot

1 cup white rice
few dried shrimps
2 dried scallops
1 egg
source : 1 tbsp each ginger extract, Chinese rice wine, 2 tbsps dark soy sauce 1 tsp sugar and 1 cup water

1 Soak dried scallops in ½ cup of water until soft. Tear scallops into shreds and set water aside.
2 Soak dried shrimps in ½ cup of water until soft. Set water aside.
3 Rinse rice and pour into clay pot. Add water from dried shrimps and scallops.
4 Cover clay pot and put on high heat until it boils. Add dried shrimps. Reset on low heat.
5 When rice is almost cooked, add dried scallop shreds.
6 When rice is cooked, remove from heat. Keep cover on for 15 minutes.
7 Break open an egg on top of rice. When done, serve with soy sauce and seasonings.

Add broth and pickles to the crust base and simmer to make a delicious porridge.

Thanks to Ms Evelyna Liang for the recipe.

這就是我家的出品，味道與別不同之處！

I use bamboo or winter leaves,
and we still steam them on a wood fire.
I think that's why my family's dumplings are special.

嚴家恩　祖籍開平

今天是我的結婚周年紀念日。回想起來，自結婚一個月後搬來這小社區裡，一住便四十五年了。以前這一帶多是木屋，附近有一間別墅，人是在草地上行走的。修橋補路，環境不斷變遷，大型的私人屋苑更進駐我們這小鄉村的旁邊，但是，我和我的家人仍然享受到及呼吸到清新的空氣！雖然小鄉村的衛生環境及設施比以前改善了不少，可是，我仍然記得夫妻二人怎樣從「零」開始。1950年，我從大陸來到香港。及後在織布廠當女工，工餘連飯也來不及進食，便要趕往學校，繼續那在鄉間未完成的小學課程。後來要返夜班，才停止上夜學。可是，人生的學習，怎會局限於課堂之內呢？剛結婚，除了二人的互相適應外，同時需要嘗試新的生活模式——種菜、養豬的務農生活。日出而作，日入而息；肩膊上擯抬「豬餿水」，村民交換飼養、種植的心得，就如趕赴墟期般，場面熱鬧非常，如今歷歷在目，儼如昨天的事。廣東新興人都喜歡在五月節或新年期間包糉子，就如北方人喜包餃子一般。我在鄰家嬸嬸的悉心教導下，學會了包那方形的【新興糉子】。每次看見我的姪子、姪女及他們的下一代，下箸如飛的情況，以及他們的滿足神情，總叫我的心情比那糉子裡的香糯還要暖意綿綿。他們常說只此一家，在別處是吃不到的。除我和丈夫累積四十多年的實戰經驗外，那用來包裹糯米的葉子，也是自家栽種出來的竹葉或冬葉。還有，到目前為止，我們仍然以柴火來烹煮糉子。我想這就是我家的出品，味道與別不同之處！在今天，這特別的一天，除了種種花、除除雜草外，心裡不時細味著這些年來的生活片段，不禁使我有感而發。食物——除了為我們帶來溫飽外，亦為鄰居、親戚、朋友、夫妻之間，帶來互相合作、互相分享的機會，更可為生活加添樂趣，或成為彼此的溝通藝術呢！感謝！感謝！這上天賜下的「糧源」及良緣！

在農村沒有什麼超級市場，但一個社區中通常至少會有一個墟市，販賣各式蔬菜、雞、魚等商品。墟市不是每天24小時一年365日運作的，只在約定時日的墟期中才有，通常是秋收之後。

Today is my wedding anniversary. I remember the day when we moved here to this small community in Sau Mau Ping one month after getting married. That was forty-five years ago. This place used to be full of wooden homes. There was a mansion nearby. The people who lived there walked on the grass. It has all changed so much, and housing complexes have now

been built next to our village. However, my family and I still manage to enjoy the tranquillity and the fresh air. I arrived in Hong Kong in 1950 from the mainland and got a job in a textiles factory. I used to skip dinner to attend evening school to complete my primary studies, which I hadn't been able to do on the mainland, but I had to stop going to night school when I started doing night shifts. But learning isn't confined to the classroom. Shortly after we got married, my husband and I decided to try our hand at farming: growing vegetables and tending livestock. We started work early every morning and finished late every night. The villagers would mingle and exchange information about farming. It was always boisterous and jolly. I can still see it in my mind as if it happened just yesterday. People from Xinxing like to make squared-shaped Zongzi sticky rice dumplings during the May Festival [Tuen Ng or Dragon Boat Festival] and Chinese New Year—just as those from the north like to make dumplings. An old woman who lived next door patiently taught me how to make Xinxing-style dumplings. When I see my nephews and nieces gulp them down, I feel a surge of warmth in my heart. I use bamboo or winter leaves, and we still steam them on a wood fire. I think that's why my family's dumplings are special. Sometimes, these memories surge back—and with them, my emotions. Food brings us not just a full stomach, but also the opportunity to cooperate and share with our neighbours, relatives and friends. Food enriches our lives and becomes a way of communicating. It is heaven's gift of *leung yuen* [meaning "source of food" and sounds like "blessed serendipity" in Cantonese].

新興大糉（約10隻分量）

糯米約960克
開邊綠豆約480克
腩肉450克
乾栗子200克
臘腸、大蝦米各120克
冬葉約30-40塊，竹葉約20-30塊
水草一扎
醃料：鹽1茶匙，五香粉1/2茶匙，胡椒粉適量

預備

1 熱水浸乾栗子過夜，沖洗後瀝乾水分
2 煲滾水，放冬葉入內略煮片刻，取出沖水後再用清水浸軟，及去除葉的苦澀味。重複兩次，瀝乾水分
3 竹葉、水草泡熱水浸軟，瀝乾水分
4 糯米泡洗5-6次，瀝乾水分，加入少許鹽拌勻
5 先浸開邊綠豆數小時，然後泡洗4-5次，瀝乾水分，加入少許鹽拌勻
6 腩肉洗淨，切小塊，下醃料，醃30分鐘
7 臘腸切小段
8 熱水浸大蝦米片刻，泡洗5-6次，瀝乾水分

做法

1 將2塊竹葉，十字形的放在碟的中央，跟著把2片冬葉排放在上面
2 抓一把糯米，放在冬葉面，鋪平
3 抓一把開邊綠豆，放糯米上，鋪平
4 將腩肉、臘腸、大蝦米、乾栗子等餡料（分量隨意）排放在中央
5 鋪上一層薄薄的糯米，然後蓋上1片冬葉
6 將冬葉、竹葉用手壓實，把左右兩邊所有葉子覆向中央包緊，跟著將首、尾之所有葉子向中央覆裹包緊，收口要向上
7 用水草「井」字形把糉子包紮好
8 將裹好的糉放入鍋內，注熱水浸過糉面，煮3小時便可食用。煮糉時要補充沸水，避免燒乾水分

進食時，蘸以白糖或豉油

Zongzi (Sticky Rice Dumplings) from Xinxing (makes 10 dumplings)

960 g glutinous rice, pinch salt
480 g split mung beans
450 g pork belly
200 g dried chestnuts
120 g Chinese sausage
120 g large dried shrimp
30 - 40 sheets winter melon leaves
20 - 30 sheets bamboo leaves
straw or string for tying the dumplings
marinade for pork belly : 1 tsp salt, ½ tsp five-spice powder, pepper to taste

Preparation

1 Soak chestnuts in hot water overnight. Wash and drain.
2 Place winter melon leaves in boiling water for a minute, then rinse. Soak in clean water; repeat twice until leaves are soft. Wipe dry.
3 Blanch bamboo leaves and straw and soak until soft. Wipe dry.
4 Wash and drain glutinous rice five to six times. Drain. Add a little salt and mix well.
5 Soak split mung beans for a few hours. Wash and drain four to five times. Drain. Add a little salt and mix well.
6 Wash pork belly and cut into small pieces. Marinate for 30 minutes.
7 Cut Chinese sausage into thin slices.
8 Soak dried shrimps in hot water. Wash five to six times. Drain.

Directions

1 Place two bamboo leaves in the shape of a cross on a plate. Place two winter leaves on top.
2 Put a handful of glutinous rice on the leaves and flatten.
3 Spread a handful of mung beans on top of the rice.
4 Put some pork belly, Chinese sausage, dried shrimp and chestnuts in the centre of the dumplings. The amount of filling depends on your taste.
5 Cover with a thin layer of glutinous rice, then put a sheet of winter leaves on top.
6 Press down the ingredients firmly. Fold the opposite sides of bamboo leaves together around the rice ball and wrap it tightly to form a square, ensuring that the opening faces upward.
7 Tie the dumpling with straw or string two times on each side in the shape of the Chinese character 井, meaning a well.
8 In a large saucepan, cover the dumplings with hot water and boil for three hours. Continually refill the saucepan with boiling water to prevent the dumplings from burning or drying up.

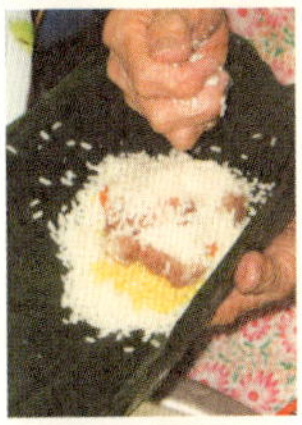

Serve with sugar or soy sauce for dipping.

食譜索引 Recipe Index

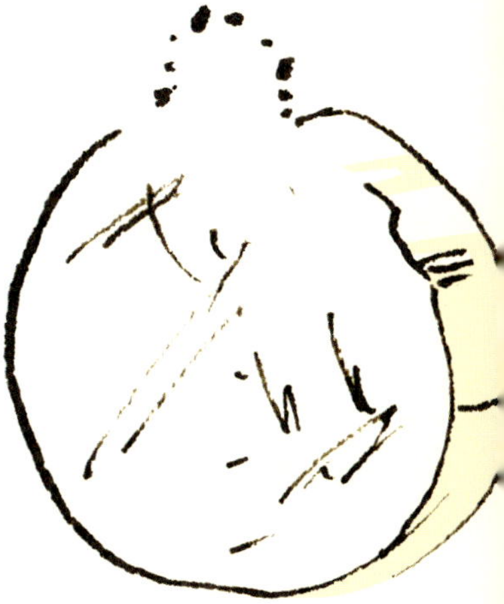

回味 I Taste

致謝　Thank You

老爹媽思廚項目有賴以下機構及人士協助及支持，全人藝動謹此致謝。

Art for All would like to thank the following organizations and people for their support and help with the research and publishing of this book.

李玉蘭 Audrey Lee
Janet Wong Chang Sui Kum
Julie Kong Wai Ming
Mimee Cheung Wan
Ponti Trading Limited
Regina Chu
Spencer Lee & Company
Wimmie Cheung Wan May

「**全人藝動**」為註冊慈善藝術團體，成立於2001年，旨在協助因社會、經濟或身體等條件限制，而失去接觸藝術機會的弱勢社群。

Art for All is a non-profit Community Art Charitable Organization founded in 2001 which enables socially underprivileged people to encounter the arts. Target groups include people who are (publicly) deprived of these opportunities due to different social, economic or physical limitations. Art for All facilitates individuals to recognize their creative potential, develop their confidence and skills, and encourage integration with the community as a whole.

鄰舍輔導會本著誠信、希望與愛心，自1968年起致力為香港市民提供卓越而專業的社會服務。成立初期，鄰舍輔導會以提供諮詢輔導服務為主，後為更適切地回應社會需要，服務範圍及對象漸趨多元化，近年更將服務推展至內地。展望將來，鄰舍輔導會將本著創會精神，與市民共同締造一個互相關懷、尊重及分享的社會。

The Neighbourhood Advice-Action Council (NAAC), a multi-service non-government organization in Hong Kong, delivers professional services, encourages self-help and mutual support, promotes social equity and justice, and works to develop a caring and sharing society. Established in 1968, NAAC originally advised and counselled. In 1974, in response to the growth in demand for community development, the NAAC directed its services for the most vulnerable residents in Hong Kong, regardless of age and social status. In 1992, the NAAC was transformed into an organization rendering services for children, youth, adults, elderly, disabled persons and families; in 1998, services began in Mainland China.

老爹媽思廚
GRANDMA GRANDPA COOK

簡亦樂MCCM Creations | www.mccmcreations.com
二零一零年四月 初版 First published April 2010
二零一零年七月 初版二刷 Reprint edition July 2010

概念 Concept | 梁以瑚 Evelyna Liang
攝影 Photography | Michael Wolf, 梁以瑚 Evelyna Liang
主編 Chief Editor | 楊陽Yeung Yang
編輯團隊 Editorial Team | 方俞 Kristy Fong, 思樂維 Madeleine Marie Slavick, Ned Lydon, 黃宇鵬 Wong Yu Pang (小土 Siu To)
設計 Design & Artwork | 吳嘉妍 Diana Ng, 王紫盈 Michelle Wong, 何義權 Ho Yee Kuen
插圖 Illustration | 吳嘉妍 Diana Ng

全人藝動於2003-2006年舉辦了「戲膳藝傳」活動，現將有關內容重新審訂演繹，結集成書。全人藝動工作組全力支援是項研究工作及資料整理。

This book project is inspired by an event L'Art et Le Chef organized by Art For All in 2003-2006. The research and the organization of the materials are supported by Art for All work team:
梁以瑚 Evelyna Liang, 黃宇鵬 Wong Yu Pang (小土 Siu To), 蘇慧盈 Wylie So, 王基信 Samson Wong, 嚴婉芬 Esther Yim, 張雲美美 Mimee Cheung, 黃儀娟 Cecilia Ting, 黃立暄 Jessica Huang, 崔雪梅 Connie Tsui, 符榮師 Mig Fu, Michael Wolf, 小西 Tiny West, 阿飯 Fandy Fan, 簡仲宜 Joey Kan, 鄭敏 Sheila Cheng

ISBN 978-988-18583-9-9 paperback